Tax Policy Reforms in the OECD 2016

This work is published under the responsibility of the Secretary-General of the OECD. The opinions expressed and arguments employed herein do not necessarily reflect the official views of OECD member countries.

This document and any map included herein are without prejudice to the status of or sovereignty over any territory, to the delimitation of international frontiers and boundaries and to the name of any territory, city or area.

Please cite this publication as:
OECD (2016), *Tax Policy Reforms in the OECD 2016*, OECD Publishing, Paris.
http://dx.doi.org/10.1787/9789264260399-en

ISBN 978-92-64-26037-5 (print)
ISBN 978-92-64-26039-9 (PDF)

The statistical data for Israel are supplied by and under the responsibility of the relevant Israeli authorities. The use of such data by the OECD is without prejudice to the status of the Golan Heights, East Jerusalem and Israeli settlements in the West Bank under the terms of international law.

Latvia was not an OECD member at the time of preparation of this publication. Accordingly, Latvia does not appear in the list of OECD members and is not included in the area totals.

Photo credits: Cover image word cloud ©Tagul.com

Corrigenda to OECD publications may be found on line at: *www.oecd.org/about/publishing/corrigenda.htm*.

Foreword

This is the first edition of *Tax Policy Reforms in the OECD.* This annual series of reports aims to track tax policy developments over time across OECD countries. This year's edition provides an overview of tax reforms in 2015. It identifies the most significant tax policy reforms that were implemented, legislated or announced in 2015 as well as common tax policy trends across groups of countries. Monitoring tax policy reforms across the OECD and understanding the context in which they were undertaken is crucial to inform tax policy discussions as well as to support member and non-member countries in their assessment and design of future tax reforms.

This report was produced by the Tax Policy and Statistics Division of the Centre for Tax Policy and Administration. It was led by Sarah Perret and written jointly with Florens Flues, Tibor Hanappi and Pierce O'Reilly under the supervision of Bert Brys. The authors would like to thank the delegates of Working Party No. 2 on Tax Policy Analysis and Tax Statistics (WP2) and the Committee on Fiscal Affairs (CFA) for their inputs. The authors would also like to acknowledge David Bradbury, Tom Neubig, Kurt Van Dender and Piet Battiau for their valuable comments and suggestions, and Michael Sharratt for his technical support with the questionnaires and database.

Table of contents

Figures

Tables

Boxes

Executive summary

In a context of low growth, subdued investment, high unemployment and inequality, tax policy plays an important role in supporting both economic growth and greater inclusiveness. Tax policies have direct implications on economic growth as well as on how the benefits of growth are shared across the population. They also play a significant *indirect* role in supporting inclusive growth through their capacity to finance growth- and equity-friendly public expenditures such as investment in education and infrastructure.

This report provides an overview of the tax reforms that were introduced in OECD countries in 2015. It identifies the most significant tax policy reforms that were implemented, legislated or announced in 2015 as well as common tax policy trends across groups of countries. The discussion in the report is primarily based on member countries' responses to the OECD Tax Policy Reform Questionnaire which is sent yearly to all member countries to collect information on tax reforms and their expected revenue effects. The paper aims to inform tax policy discussions and to support countries in their assessment and design of tax reforms.

The report finds that tax reforms shifted towards a focus on growth. While tax reforms were largely motivated by fiscal consolidation objectives following the crisis, encouraging growth seems to have been the main objective of tax reforms in 2015. Across all OECD countries, many of the reforms focused on reducing taxes on labour and corporate income, with partial revenue increases or shifts towards consumption and environmentally related taxes. In addition, a number of the post-crisis tax policy trends, which had often been a response to fiscal consolidation imperatives, seem to be coming to an end. In particular, the continual increases in labour taxes and value-added tax (VAT) rates which had been observed in the years following the crisis stopped and may even be reversing. With regard to corporate income tax (CIT), rate reductions had generally slowed down after the crisis but seem to be picking up again.

Major international developments in the area of taxation in 2015 have also influenced tax policy reforms in OECD countries. Many of the reported CIT and VAT reforms reflected the impact of the adoption of the recommendations agreed upon as part of the OECD/G20 Base Erosion and Profit Shifting (BEPS) project and the endorsement of the OECD International VAT/GST Guidelines.

The report shows that Austria, Belgium, Greece, Japan, the Netherlands, Norway and Spain implemented, legislated or announced the most comprehensive tax reforms in 2015. In Austria, Belgium and the Netherlands, the main objective was to reduce taxes on labour income. In Norway and Japan, a key consideration was to support investment through a reduction in corporate taxes. Spain's tax reform involved both corporate and labour tax cuts to boost the economy. However, not all of these reforms appeared to be revenue neutral, raising some concerns about their ongoing sustainability. Finally, Greece introduced significant reforms, in particular in the areas of VAT and CIT, as part of its bailout agreement.

More specifically, the report found that:

- **In 2015, the tax wedge on labour income stabilised after years of steady increases. However, many of the reforms legislated or announced in 2015 and coming into effect in 2016 point to a trend of declining tax burdens on labour income.** A significant number of these reforms focused on reducing tax burdens on low-income taxpayers and households with children through rate cuts and increases in tax allowances and credits.
- **Several countries raised tax rates on dividends and other sources of personal capital income**. The increase in statutory tax rates on capital income, both since the crisis and over the last year, could be a response to a renewed focus on inequality and the differential tax treatment between labour and capital income.
- **The trend of CIT rate reductions, which had slowed down after the crisis, seems to be gaining renewed momentum.** Five OECD countries implemented or legislated general CIT rate reductions in 2015 and four have announced CIT rate cuts in the coming years.
- **Several countries introduced CIT base-broadening measures, in particular to protect domestic tax bases against tax avoidance by multinational enterprises**. In response to the recommendations agreed upon as part of the OECD/G20 BEPS project, a number of countries enacted specific anti-avoidance legislation.
- **The increase in standard VAT rates, which had been a clear trend since the end of the crisis until the beginning of 2015, did not continue over the course of 2015.** In many countries, increases in VAT revenues are expected from reducing the scope of reduced rates and tax compliance improvements. However, a number of countries narrowed VAT bases by expanding the use of reduced rates.
- **Environmentally related tax reform in 2015 was limited mostly to changes in taxes on energy use and cars.** As a result, the environmental effectiveness of taxes was somewhat improved and revenues are expected to grow in some countries in the short term.
- **There were only a limited number of reforms in the area of property taxes**. In addition, the trends across OECD countries were unclear, with some countries raising property tax burdens and others lowering them. This seems to suggest that the potential to raise revenues in an efficient way through property taxes, especially through recurrent taxes on residential property, is not being fully exploited.

Chapter 1

Introducing the first edition of *Tax Policy Reforms in the OECD*

This chapter provides a brief introduction to the first edition of Tax Policy Reforms in the OECD*. It explains the purpose of this new annual series of reports as well as the methodology and process upon which they are based.*

In a context of sluggish global growth, subdued investment, high unemployment and rising inequality levels, tax policy plays an important role in supporting both economic growth and greater inclusiveness. Tax policies have direct implications on economic growth (OECD, 2010) as well as on how the benefits of growth are shared across the population (Brys et al., forthcoming). They also play a significant *indirect* role in supporting inclusive growth through their capacity to finance growth- and equity-friendly public expenditures such as investment in education and infrastructure (OECD, 2015; Cournède et al., 2014).

This report is the first edition of *Tax Policy Reforms in the OECD*. This annual series of reports aims to track tax policy developments over time across OECD countries. This year's edition provides an overview of tax reforms in 2015. It identifies the most significant tax policy reforms that were implemented, legislated or announced in 2015 as well as common tax policy trends across groups of countries. The paper aims to inform tax policy discussions and to support countries in their assessment and design of future tax reforms.

The discussion in this report is primarily based on member countries' responses to the 2016 Annual Tax Policy Reform Questionnaire which requested information on tax reforms that were implemented, legislated or announced during calendar year 2015. The questionnaire asked member countries to describe these tax measures and to provide details on their expected revenue implications and other relevant information, including the rationale for the measures (see Box 1.1).

Box 1.1. The OECD Annual Tax Policy Reform Questionnaire

At the Working Party No. 2 on Tax Policy Analysis and Tax Statistics (WP2) meeting in November 2009, delegates from member countries agreed to start collecting more systematic information on the main tax measures adopted in each country. The motivation for this proposal was to provide consistent and comparative information on tax reforms to inform policy discussions in OECD countries.

At the November 2010 WP2 meeting, the following criteria were agreed for deciding whether a tax policy measure was sufficiently substantial to be reported in the questionnaire:

- a significant change in a tax rate;
- a change in the tax base that is expected to change revenue from that base by more than 5% or 0.1% of GDP; and
- a politically important systemic reform.

Any central or sub-central tax policy measure that was *implemented, legislated or announced* in the previous *calendar* year which meets at least one of the criteria listed above must be reported in the questionnaire.

For each reform, the questionnaire requests information on the type of tax; the dates of entry into force, legislation or announcement; the direction of the rate and/or base change; and a detailed description of the reform. The questionnaire also asks for the rationale behind the reform and estimates of the revenue impacts of the tax measures.

The 2016 questionnaire was significantly streamlined compared to previous versions. In particular, many of the fields in the questionnaire were converted into drop-down menus. The objective was to facilitate data input by member country delegates as well as data use and analysis by the OECD Secretariat.

The report is structured as follows: Chapter 2 describes the macroeconomic environment as well as recent trends in tax revenues and tax mixes in OECD countries; Chapter 3 gives an overview of the main tax policy developments in OECD countries in 2015 in each category of tax.

References

Cournède, B., A. Goujard and A. Pina (2014), "Reconciling fiscal consolidation with growth and equity", *OECD Journal: Economic Studies*, Vol. 2013/1, http://dx.doi.org/10.1787/eco_studies-2013-5jzb44vzbkhd.

Brys, B., S. Perret, A. Thomas and P. O'Reilly (forthcoming, 2016), "Tax Design for Inclusive Economic Growth", *OECD Taxation Working Papers*, OECD Publishing, Paris.

OECD (2015), *OECD Economic Outlook*, Volume 2015 Issue 2, OECD Publishing, Paris, http://dx.doi.org/10.1787/eco_outlook-v2015-2-en.

OECD (2010), *Tax Policy Reform and Economic Growth*, OECD Tax Policy Studies, No. 20, OECD Publishing, Paris, http://dx.doi.org/10.1787/9789264091085-en.

Chapter 2

Macroeconomic background and tax revenue trends

This chapter first provides an overview of recent macroeconomic developments in OECD countries, including trends in growth, productivity, investment, employment, public finances and inequality. It then describes tax revenue trends, examining both trends in total tax revenues and changes in the composition of tax revenues – i.e. tax mixes – in OECD countries. This overview of macroeconomic and tax revenue trends sets the stage for the subsequent discussion on tax policy reforms as tax policy developments are closely connected with economic trends. Indeed, tax revenues are affected by changes in macroeconomic conditions and economic developments themselves are key drivers of tax reforms.

The statistical data for Israel are supplied by and under the responsibility of the relevant Israeli authorities. The use of such data by the OECD is without prejudice to the status of the Golan Heights, East Jerusalem and Israeli settlements in the West Bank under the terms of international law.

2.1. Macroeconomic trends

The macroeconomic background covers recent trends and forecasts on growth, productivity, investment, employment, public finances and inequality. Tax policy developments are closely connected with economic trends: tax revenues are affected by changes in macroeconomic conditions and economic developments themselves are key drivers of tax reforms. This section provides background information to help understand tax revenue trends as well as tax policy changes.

Growth was slow in 2015 and is expected to remain so in 2016

Global growth was around 3% in 2015, its lowest level in the last five years. This rate is well below long-run averages and below what would be expected in a recovery phase for advanced economies and in a catching-up phase for emerging economies (OECD, 2016a). Low growth largely reflected weaknesses in emerging market economies whose growth rates declined for the fifth consecutive year (Figure 2.1). China experienced a gradual slowdown in economic activity, in particular because of the rebalancing of its economy from manufacturing to services. Deep recessions emerged in Brazil (-3.1%) and Russia (-4.0%). Fragilities in emerging markets in turn contributed to the sharp slowdown in world trade through a significant decline in their import volumes and to increased financial market uncertainty. Weak demand also contributed to the significant fall in commodity prices, hurting commodity exporters.

Figure 2.1. **Average growth rates, year-on-year percentage changes**

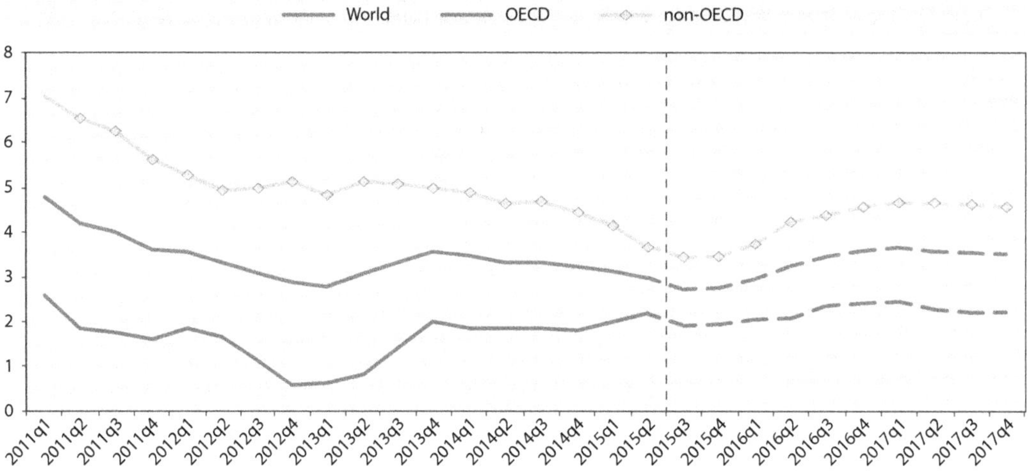

Source: OECD (2015a), "OECD Economic Outlook No. 98 (Edition 2015/2)", *OECD Economic Outlook: Statistics and Projections* (database), http://dx.doi.org/10.1787/bd810434-en.

Growth trends in OECD countries in 2015 were slightly less disappointing. The average growth rate stood at around 2%, which is much lower than the average growth rate in emerging economies but shows evidence of a modest recovery compared to previous years (Figure 2.1). This recovery was primarily helped by an improvement in private consumption (Figure 2.3). The recovery was nevertheless uneven across OECD countries with 32 of the 34 member states recording positive economic growth in 2015. Provisional growth rates ranged from -1.4% in Greece to 5.6% in Ireland in 2015 (Figure 2.2).

Figure 2.2. **Growth rates in OECD countries in 2015**

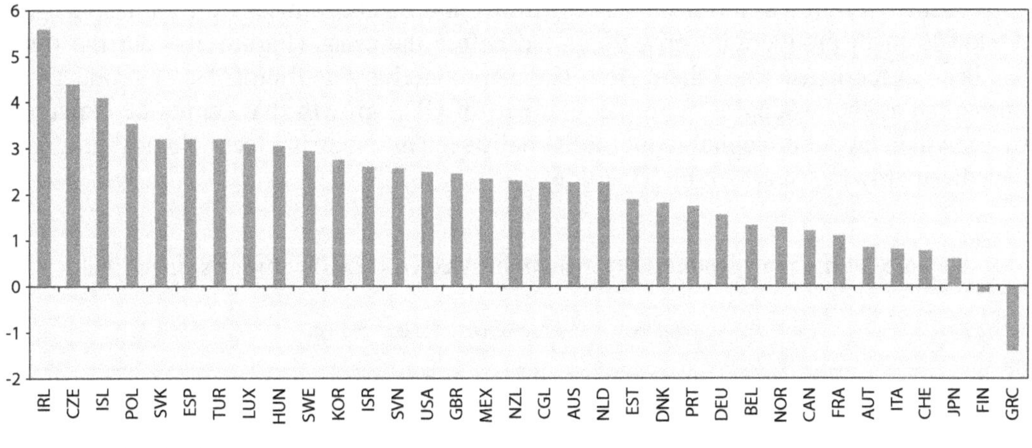

Note: Provisional values.

Source: OECD (2015a), "OECD Economic Outlook No. 98 (Edition 2015/2)", *OECD Economic Outlook: Statistics and Projections* (database), http://dx.doi.org/10.1787/bd810434-en.

Figure 2.3. **Annual % change in real private consumption expenditure, OECD weighted average**

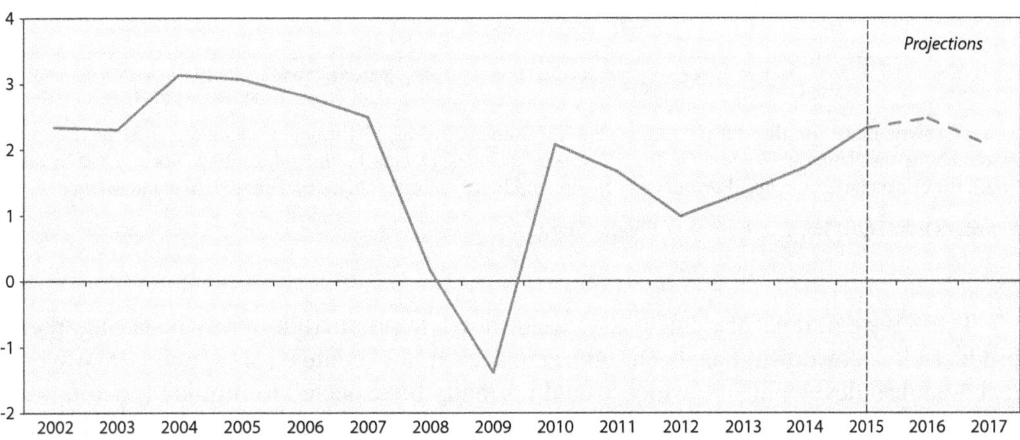

Source: OECD (2015a), "OECD Economic Outlook No. 98 (Edition 2015/2)", *OECD Economic Outlook: Statistics and Projections* (database), http://dx.doi.org/10.1787/bd810434-en.

In 2016, global growth is not expected to be higher than in 2015 due to weak trade and investment and increased financial market volatility. The latest OECD growth forecasts have been downgraded and the recovery in OECD economies is expected to remain modest. In the European Union (EU), lower oil prices have not had the expected stimulus effect on the economy and have further depressed inflation, while quantitative easing and very low interest rates have yet to generate more investment. In the United States, the recovery continues, with employment growth boosting demand, but the US economy is also facing headwinds including the negative effect of a stronger dollar on exports and lower investment in the energy sector because of low oil prices (OECD, 2016a). Meanwhile, it is expected that emerging and developing economies will generally have to face a new structural reality of slower growth rates in the future.[1] Financial instability is also a significant risk as the re-evaluation of growth prospects has led to falls in equity prices and increased volatility (OECD, 2016a).

Productivity growth has been low

Productivity growth has been slowing down in OECD countries over the last decade. A slowdown in productivity growth started before the crisis (Figure 2.4) but the trend has been exacerbated since then. Both labour productivity and multi-factor productivity (measured as the residual growth, i.e. that part of GDP growth that cannot be explained by growth in labour or capital input traditionally seen as capturing technological progress) have been growing weakly (OECD, 2015e).

Figure 2.4. **Labour productivity growth in selected OECD countries since 1990**

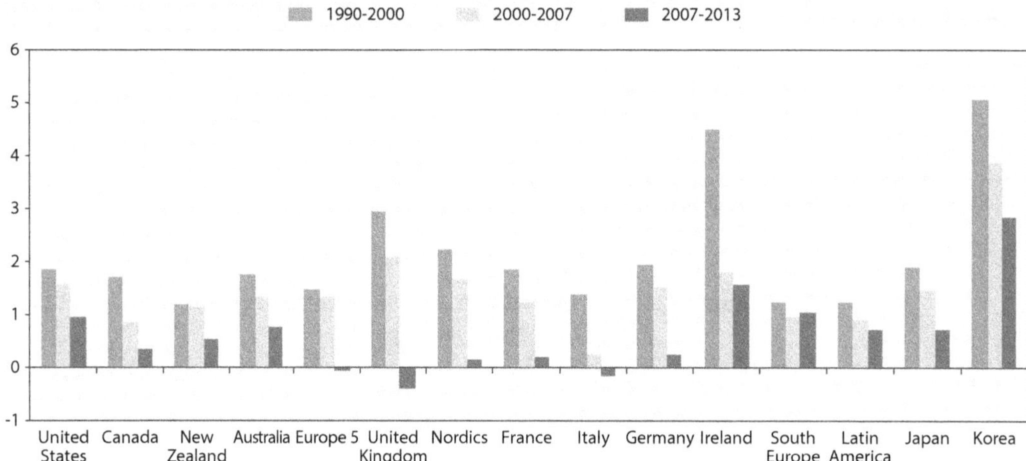

Note: Growth rates for the period ranges are the annual averages. Europe-5 includes: Austria, Belgium, Luxembourg, the Netherlands and Switzerland; Nordics includes: Denmark, Finland, Iceland, Norway and Sweden; South Europe includes: Greece, Portugal and Spain; and Latin America includes: Brazil, Chile and Mexico.

Source: OECD (2015e), *The Future of Productivity*, http://dx.doi.org/10.1787/9789264248533-en.

There is a paradoxical element to this slowdown in productivity growth. The aggregate productivity slowdown has been taking place in the context of a massive wave of technological developments, which would normally be expected to provide fresh impetus to productivity growth. Recent OECD research suggests that increased divergence between the most and least productive firms is behind the paradox of slow aggregate productivity growth despite fast technological improvements. The productivity growth slowdown appears to be not so much the result of a slower rate of innovation by the most globally advanced firms, but rather of the slower pace at which innovations spread throughout the economy, suggesting a breakdown of the "diffusion machine". Future growth will depend on reviving the forces of knowledge diffusion in particular through greater competition, innovation and labour mobility (OECD, 2015e).

Business investment remained subdued

Private capital investment fell sharply during the crisis in OECD countries and the recovery has been limited since. Although there was a very sharp drop in housing investment during the crisis, business investment accounted for most of the contraction in investment given its much larger share of total investment (IMF, 2015). Figure 2.5 shows a severe fall in private non-residential investment in the 2007-10 period, as firms reacted to weak sales by cutting capital expenditures (IMF, 2015). Between 2011 and 2015, business investment recovered slightly.

Figure 2.5. **Average annual % change in private non-residential gross fixed capital formation (volume)**

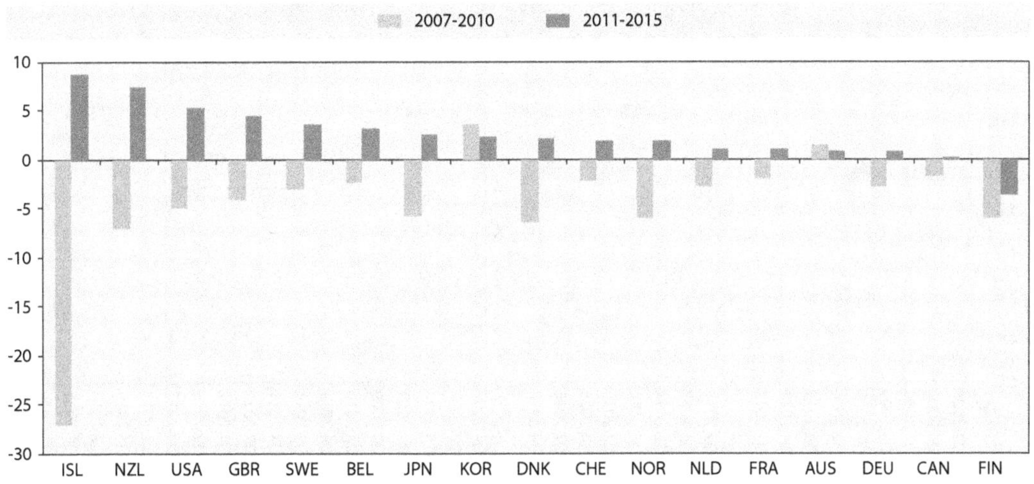

Note: Provisional values for 2015

Source: Own calculations, based on OECD (2015a), "OECD Economic Outlook No. 98 (Edition 2015/2)", *OECD Economic Outlook: Statistics and Projections* (database), http://dx.doi.org/10.1787/bd810434-en.

With regard to foreign direct investment (FDI), trends have shown a fall in inflows followed by a recent recovery in OECD countries. Global FDI inflows, which may be used to finance capital formation or cover companies' deficits and pay off loans, fell by 16% between 2013 and 2014 to USD 1.23 trillion, a level close to FDI inflows in the mid-2000s but below the pre-crisis peak of almost USD 1.9 trillion or 3.35% of world GDP in 2007. The decline in FDI flows between 2013 and 2014 was influenced mainly by the fragility of the global economy, uncertainty for investors and significant geopolitical risks. Nevertheless, trends varied across countries: developed countries saw a significant decrease while inflows to developing economies were still high by historical standards (UNCTAD, 2015). In the first half of 2015, however, the OECD experienced an increase in FDI inflows, mainly reflecting record inflows into the United States (OECD, 2015d). UNCTAD anticipates an upturn in FDI flows to USD 1.5 trillion in 2016 but significant downside risks persist including uncertainties in the Eurozone, geopolitical tensions, and persistent fragilities in emerging markets (UNCTAD, 2015).

Labour market conditions have improved but unemployment remains high in a number of countries

Labour market conditions improved in 2015 but unemployment levels remained very high in some countries, in particular in the EU. Employment growth picked up (Figure 2.6, Panel A) and unemployment rates, which had reached record levels during the crisis, started to decline, falling on average in the OECD from 8.2% in 2010 to 7.1% in the fourth quarter of 2014 (Figure 2.6, Panel B). However, the average unemployment rate at the end of 2014 was still 1.6 percentage points above its pre-crisis level (OECD, 2015b). Some countries, in particular in the EU, continued to suffer from very high unemployment levels.

Greece and Spain experienced dramatic increases in unemployment, respectively from 8.1% to 25.8% and 8.6% to 23.7% between 2007 and 2014 (Figure 2.7).

Figure 2.6. **Average employment growth (Panel A) and unemployment rates in the OECD, Euro area and the United States (Panel B)**

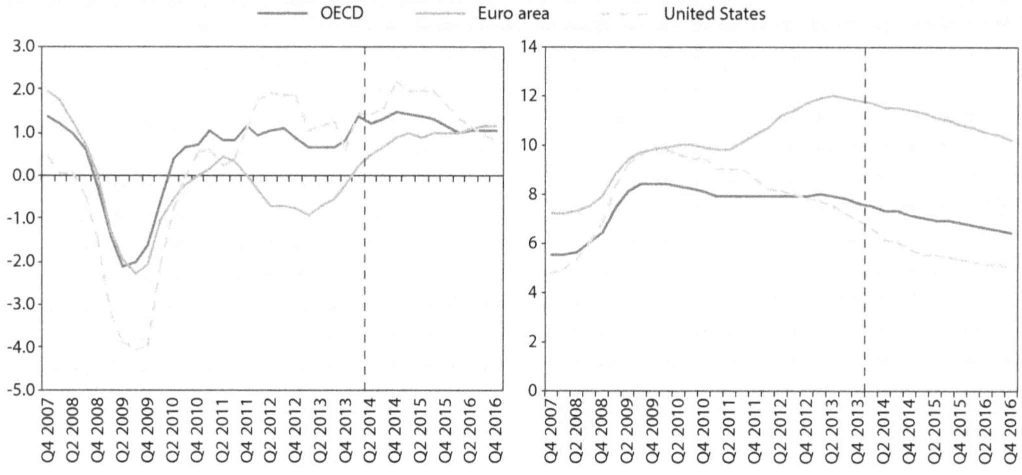

Figure 2.7. **Unemployment rates in OECD countries, % of the labour force**

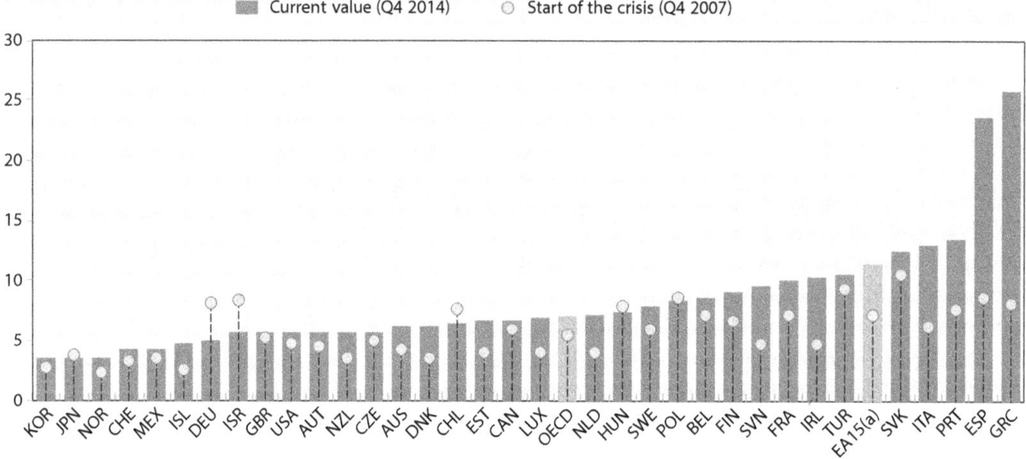

Note: (a) Aggregate of 15 OECD countries of the euro area.

Source: OECD (2015b), OECD Employment Outlook, http://dx.doi.org/10.1787/empl_outlook-2015-en.

While labour market conditions are expected to continue improving, unemployment, particularly for the long-term unemployed and youth, will remain a priority concern in many countries. Long-term unemployment remains at record levels. For the OECD area as a whole, more than one in three unemployed individuals had been out of work for 12 months or more in the fourth quarter of 2014. The size of this group has increased by 77.2% since 2007. There is a danger that a number of these long-term unemployed have become completely disconnected from the labour market, making it harder to reduce unemployment. Youth unemployment also remains well above pre-crisis levels in many countries, reaching shares as high as 51.8% in Spain, 50.1% in Greece and 42.3% of the youth labour force in Italy in the fourth quarter of 2014 (OECD, 2015b).

Public debts reached record levels

Public debts reached historically high levels. The average OECD gross debt-to-GDP ratio stood at about 115.5% in 2014, a considerably higher level than the average debt level in 2007 of about 75% of GDP (Figure 2.8, Panel A). This substantial increase in public debt was largely due to the accumulation of fiscal deficits, the recession and specific events such as banking sector rescues (Eyraud and Wu, 2015). Across the OECD, however, there were very wide differences between countries, with public debts ranging from 13.7% of GDP in Estonia to 226.1% of GDP in Japan in 2014. Record debt levels were also reached in many European countries (e.g. Greece, Italy, Portugal, Belgium, Ireland, France, the United Kingdom and Spain) and the United States.

Figure 2.8. **General government gross debt (Panel A) and budget balance (Panel B), OECD average and range, 2000-17**

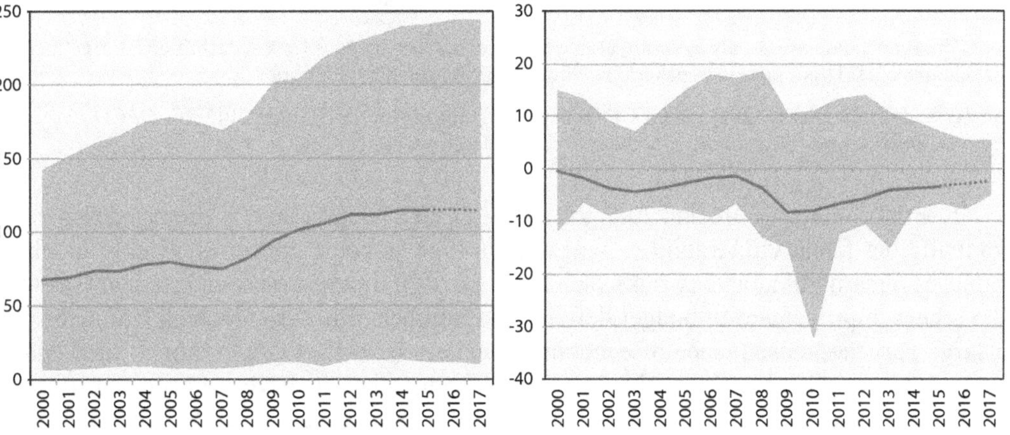

Note: Projections after 2014

Source: Data from OECD (2015a), "OECD Economic Outlook No. 98 (Edition 2015/2)", *OECD Economic Outlook: Statistics and Projections* (database), http://dx.doi.org/10.1787/bd810434-en.

Budget deficits narrowed but remained larger than in the pre-crisis period. Concerns about high and rising public debt levels led to substantial fiscal consolidation efforts, especially in 2011 and 2012, and to a lesser extent in 2013. In 2014, budget positions ranged between a deficit of 7.7% of GDP in Japan and a surplus of 9.1% of GDP in Norway, while the OECD average stood at a deficit of 3.8% of GDP. These deficits are narrower than during the crisis years – in particular compared to 2009 when the average deficit in the OECD reached 8.4% of GDP – but remain larger than pre-crisis levels (Figure 2.8, Panel B).

Public debts and budget deficits are mutually reinforcing (Figure 2.9). On the one hand, rising deficits result in higher public debts. On the other hand, interest payments must be paid on debt, so larger debts mean that a larger share of future budgets has to be devoted to paying interest. Interest rates on new debt can also go up in response to rising debt and deficits, increasing the costs of servicing debt. Nevertheless, the demand for government debt can be more or less sensitive to countries' levels of indebtedness depending on various factors. For instance, the demand for US Treasury bonds tends to be less sensitive to the government's level of debt than in European countries, in part because of the country's position in the world economy.

Figure 2.9. **Gross government debt and deficit levels as a % of GDP in OECD countries in 2014**

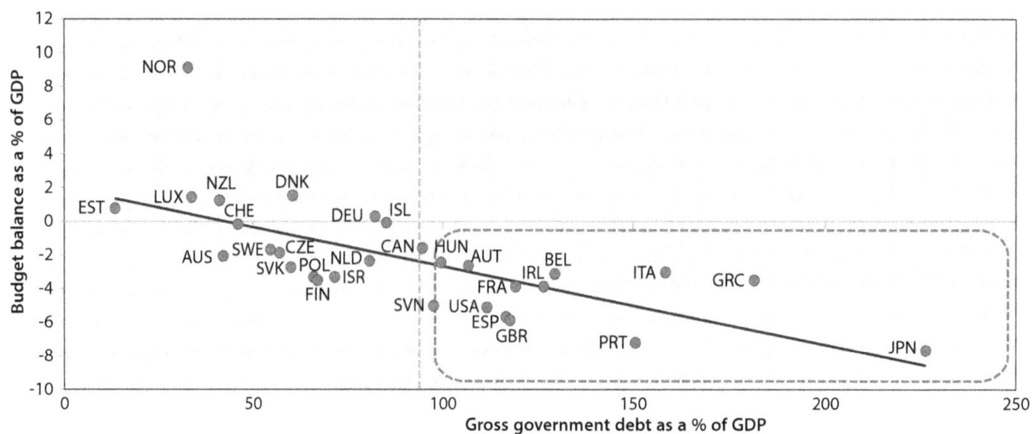

Note: Gross debt data are not always comparable across countries due to different definitions or treatment of debt components. This figure uses general government gross financial liabilities.

Source: Data from OECD (2015a), "OECD Economic Outlook No. 98 (Edition 2015/2)", *OECD Economic Outlook: Statistics and Projections* (database), http://dx.doi.org/10.1787/bd810434-en.

Over the course of 2016 and 2017, the average OECD deficit level is projected to narrow gradually but fiscal vulnerabilities will remain high in some countries. Highly indebted countries remain vulnerable to risks such as increases in interest rates and stagnant growth. The recent improvement in budget deficits in a number of highly indebted countries was in large part the consequence of economic recovery (e.g. Portugal, Spain, United States and Ireland). In other highly indebted countries, budget deficits have not been significantly reduced (e.g. France, Belgium) or have increased (e.g. Greece due to the recapitalisation of the banking sector). In the absence of more structural reforms, public debts are not expected to decrease significantly and fiscal vulnerabilities will remain high in these countries in the coming years.

In a number of other OECD countries, fiscal sustainability risks are much lower. Fiscal positions are expected to remain sustainable in Scandinavian countries. Germany recorded a general government budget surplus of 0.4% in 2014 and its debt-to-GDP ratio is projected to fall gradually in the coming years. Central European countries have seen a deterioration of their public finances but debt levels remain comparatively low (with the exception of Slovenia and Hungary) and budget deficits are expected to narrow again in the next two years. In Australia and New Zealand, despite increases in public debts since the crisis, debt-to-GDP ratios are still sound. Finally, in emerging OECD countries, fiscal positions are expected to remain sustainable even if fiscal space is narrowing.

Inequality is high by historical standards

Inequality in OECD countries is high by historical standards. The average Gini coefficient in the OECD reached about 0.32 in 2013, a 10% or 3 point increase compared to its level in the mid-1980s (OECD, 2015c). The global economic crisis reinforced income inequality mainly through the decline in employment. In the 27 countries for which data is available, 19 experienced an increase in market income (i.e. before taxes and transfers) inequality between 2008 and 2012 (Figure 2.10). Inequality in the distribution of wealth has also increased over recent decades and is in fact much greater than income inequality as assets are much more concentrated than income (OECD, 2015c).

Figure 2.10. **Percentage point changes between market income Gini coefficients between 2008 and 2012**

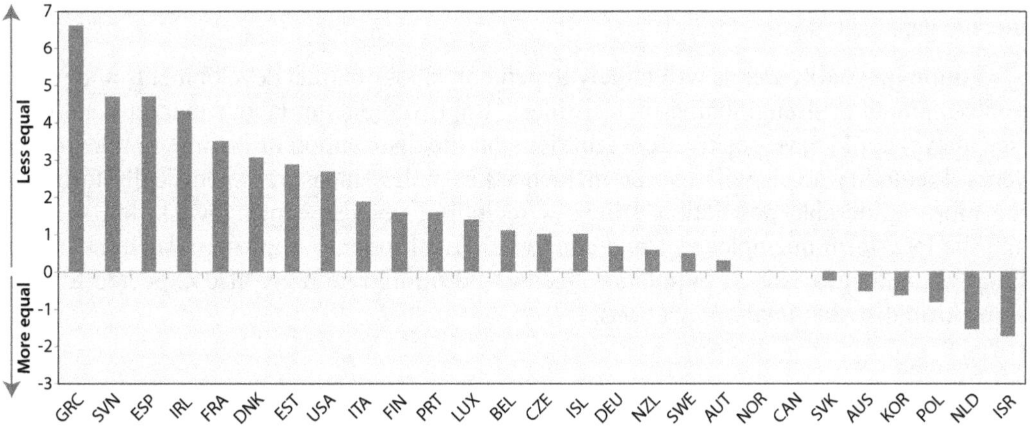

Less equal
More equal
7 6 5 4 3 2 1 0 -1 -2 -3
GRC SVN ESP IRL FRA DNK EST USA ITA FIN PRT LUX BEL CZE ISL DEU NZL SWE AUT NOR CAN SVK AUS KOR POL NLD ISR

Note: Data not available for all countries. 2011 data for Canada.

Source: OECD (2016b), "Income distribution", *OECD Social and Welfare Statistics* (database), http://dx.doi.org/10.1787/data-00654-en.

However, countries' income inequality levels differed widely and tax and transfer systems played a varying redistributive function across the OECD. In 2012, disposable (i.e. post taxes and transfers) income inequality varied widely across countries (Figure 2.11). Some countries were characterised by low degrees of inequality, including Scandinavian and Central European countries, while others, particularly emerging OECD countries, suffered from a very unequal income distribution. These differences in disposable income inequality are explained by countries' pre-tax and transfer levels of income inequality as well as the redistributive function of their tax and transfer system. In 12 (European) OECD countries, the tax and transfer system reduced inequality by at least 40% in 2012.

Figure 2.11. **Market income, post-transfer and disposable income Gini coefficients in 2012**

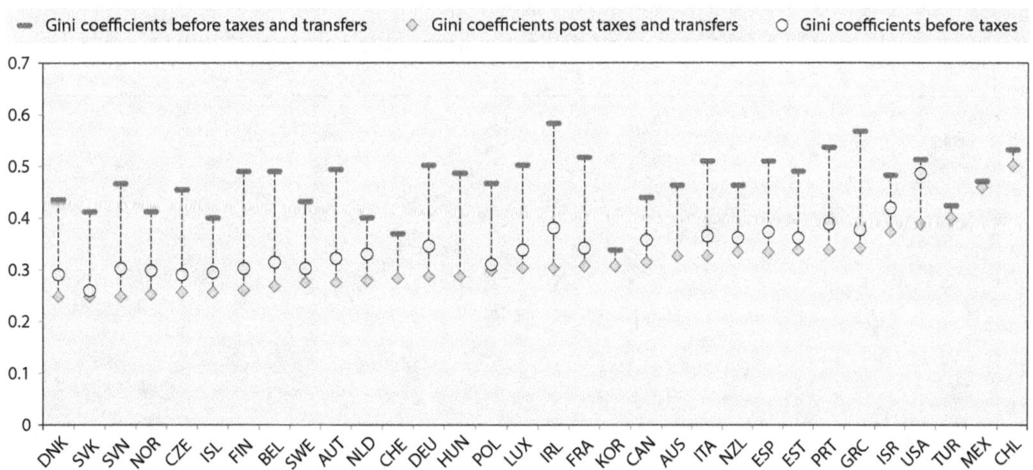

Note: No data for the UK and Japan. No data on Gini coefficients before taxes for Australia, Switzerland, Hungary, Korea, Turley Mexico and Chile. 2011 data used for Canada and Chile.

Source: OECD (2016b), "Income distribution", *OECD Social and Welfare Statistics* (database), http://dx.doi.org/10.1787/data-00654-en.

By contrast, in countries like Turkey, Mexico, Chile and Korea, taxes and transfers played a very limited redistributive role. Figure 2.11 also shows that in all OECD countries, with the notable exception of the United States, transfers play a much bigger role in narrowing income gaps than taxes.

Future inequality trends will largely depend on labour market developments and public policies aimed at strengthening inclusiveness. Improvements in labour market conditions (see above) could have positive repercussions on the distribution of income in the coming years. Inequality levels will also be influenced by policy measures specifically targeting the more vulnerable population groups – including young people, low-skilled workers and the long-term unemployed – and countries' fiscal room to implement such measures. Finally, challenges such as population ageing and immigration are also expected to have significant distributional implications.

2.2. Tax revenues trends

This section examines tax revenue trends in OECD countries – looking at both total tax-to-GDP ratios and tax mixes. The analysis looks at tax trends until 2014, the latest year for which comparable tax revenue data is available and published in the 2015 edition of *Revenue Statistics*.

The OECD average tax burden reached an all-time high in 2014

In 2014, the average tax-to-GDP ratio was the highest ever recorded since the OECD began measuring tax burdens in 1965. The average tax-to-GDP ratio reached 34.4%, a 0.2 percentage point increase from its 2013 level. Historically, average tax-to-GDP ratios increased through the 1990s, to a peak of 34.2% in 2000. They then fell slightly between 2001 and 2004, but rose again between 2005 and 2007. With the crisis, tax revenues dropped sharply. In 2009, the OECD average tax revenues were down to 32.7% of GDP, partly as a result of automatic stabilisers and various discretionary measures that several countries had adopted to stimulate economic activity. Since then, the average tax-to-GDP ratio has continually increased (Figure 2.12).

Figure 2.12. **OECD tax-to-GDP ratio, unweighted average, 2000-14**

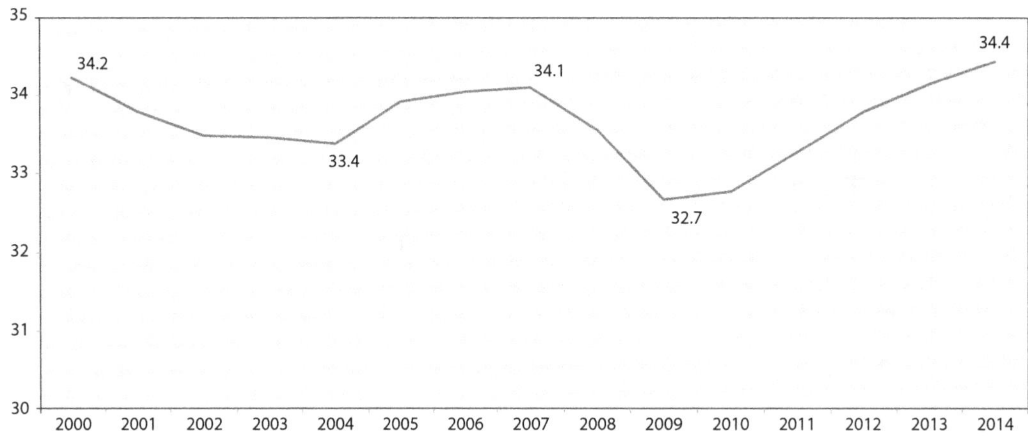

Source: OECD (2015), *Revenue Statistics 2015*, http://dx.doi.org/10.1787/rev_stats-2015-en-fr.

Tax burdens varied considerably across OECD countries in 2014, ranging from below 20% to more than 50% of GDP (Figure 2.13). Denmark was the country with the highest tax-to-GDP ratio (50.9%), followed by France (45.2%) and Belgium (44.7%). The countries with the lowest tax burdens were Mexico (19.5%) and Chile (19.8%). They were followed by Korea (24.6%) and the United States which had a tax-to-GDP ratio of 26% in 2014.

Figure 2.13. **Tax-to-GDP ratios by country in 2014**

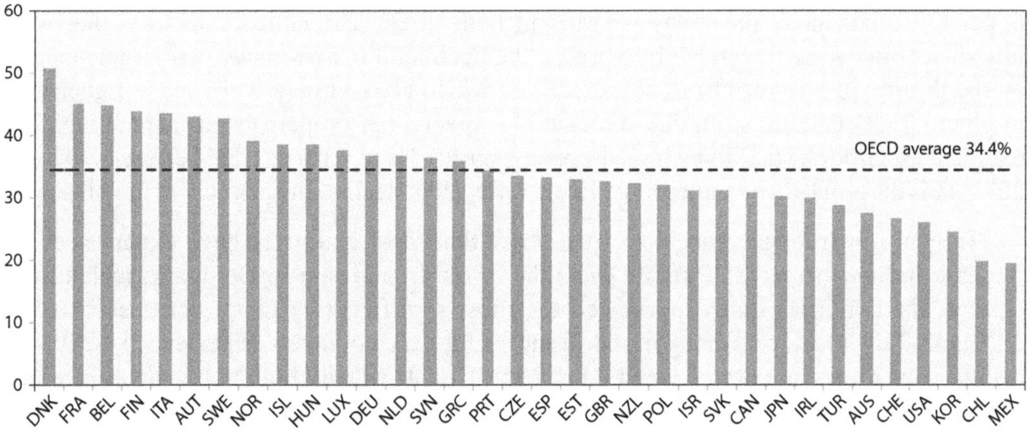

Note: No 2014 data for Australia, Japan, the Netherlands and Poland. The data for Germany was revised since the publication of *Revenue Statistics 2015.*

Source: OECD (2015), *Revenue Statistics 2015*, http://dx.doi.org/10.1787/rev_stats-2015-en-fr.

Changes in revenues between 2013 and 2014 also differed across countries (Figure 2.14). The largest tax ratio increases between 2013 and 2014 were recorded in Denmark (3.3 percentage points explained by an increase in taxes on income and profits as a % of GDP) and Iceland (2.8 p.p., due to higher revenues from taxes on goods and services and taxes on income and profits). Other countries experiencing substantial revenue increases included Greece (1.5 p.p.), Estonia (1.1 p.p.) and New Zealand (1.0 p.p.). The largest revenue falls were recorded in Norway (1.4 p.p.; due to a decline in taxes on income and profits) and the Czech Republic (0.8 p.p., due to a decline in taxes on goods and services). These

Figure 2.14. **Changes in tax-to-GDP ratios between 2013 and 2014, in percentage points**

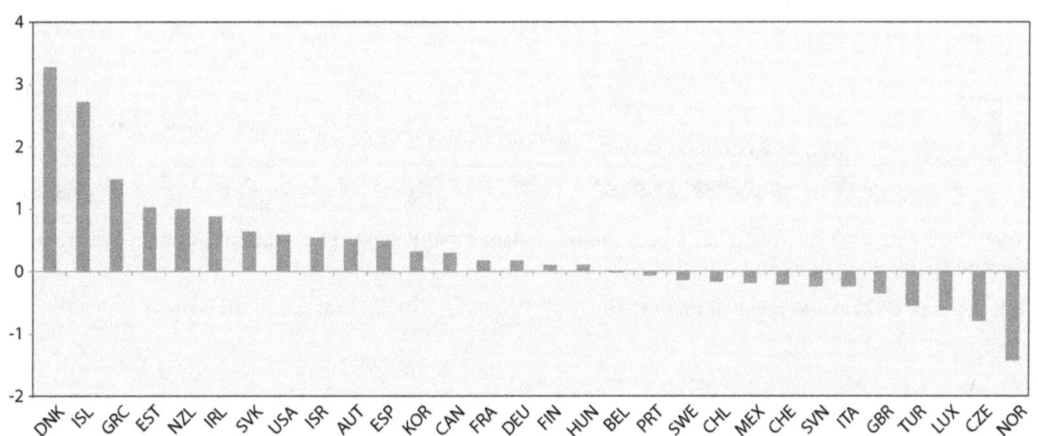

Note: No 2014 data for Australia, Japan, the Netherlands and Poland. The data for Germany was revised since the publication of *Revenue Statistics 2015.*

Source: OECD (2015), *Revenue Statistics 2015*, http://dx.doi.org/10.1787/rev_stats-2015-en-fr.

countries were followed by Luxembourg and Turkey, which experienced revenue falls of around 0.6 percentage points.

Tax revenue changes result from both policy choices and changes in macroeconomic variables such as consumption, employment or profits and their effects on tax bases. Some of the factors that may explain the most significant revenue changes are discussed here. In the case of Denmark, the revenue increase was in part generated by one-off revenues from the restructuring of the taxation of pension saving schemes.[2] In Iceland, the rise in revenues is partly explained by the many reforms in both direct and indirect taxation that were introduced following the crisis. In Norway, the decline in tax revenues was largely caused by the decline in revenues from corporate tax, which are comparatively much higher than in other OECD countries (mainly because of a special tax on petroleum income which is recorded as corporate tax) but which dropped from 10.3% to 7.1% of GDP between 2012 and 2014. This drop in CIT revenues most likely reflected a decline in earnings in the oil sector.

Trends over a longer period of time show that most countries have experienced an increase in their tax-to-GDP ratios since the crisis. In addition to Denmark, Iceland and Greece, the countries that experienced the most significant revenue increases between 2010 and 2014 included Portugal and France. Only six countries experienced a revenue decrease over the same period (see Figure 2.15). Countries with high public debts after the crisis generally experienced greater increases in their tax-to-GDP ratios although there were some exceptions (Figure 2.16, Panel A). In addition, Figure 2.16 (Panel B) shows that there was a slightly negative correlation between total tax revenues as a share of GDP in 2010 and the percentage change in tax revenues between 2010 and 2014, suggesting a slight convergence trend in tax-to-GDP ratios across OECD countries. However, more work would be needed to examine tax revenue convergence patterns across OECD countries.

Figure 2.15. **Changes in tax-to-GDP ratios between 2010 and 2014, in percentage points**

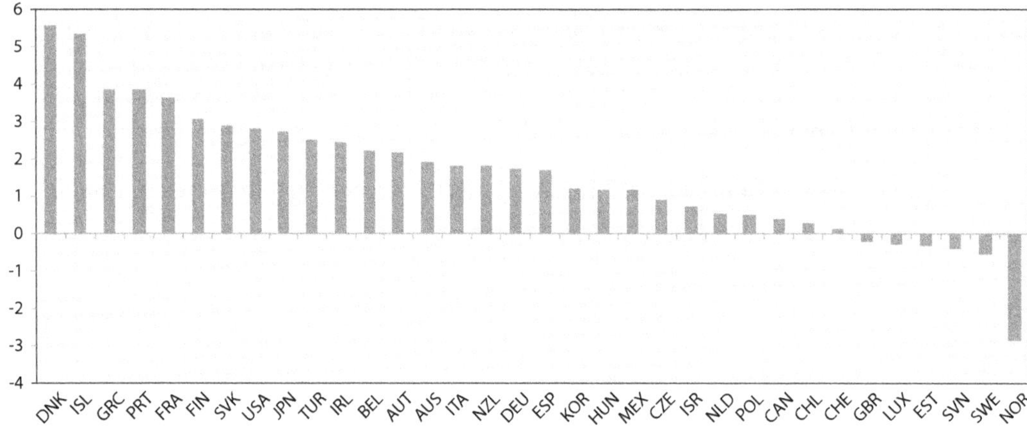

Note: 2013 data used for Australia, Japan, the Netherlands and Poland. The data for Germany was revised since the publication of *Revenue Statistics 2015*.

Source: OECD (2015), *Revenue Statistics 2015*, http://dx.doi.org/10.1787/rev_stats-2015-en-fr.

Figure 2.16. **Gross government debt and tax revenue changes (Panel A) and tax revenue convergence (Panel B)**

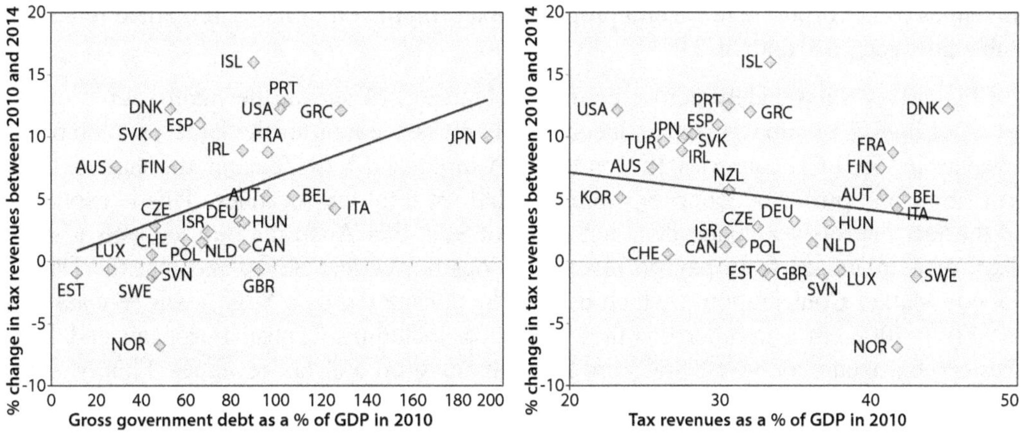

Sources: Data from OECD (2015), *Revenue Statistics 2015*, http://dx.doi.org/10.1787/rev_stats-2015-en-fr, and OECD (2015a), "OECD Economic Outlook No. 98 (Edition 2015/2)", *OECD Economic Outlook: Statistics and Projections* (database), http://dx.doi.org/10.1787/bd810434-en.

The average tax mix shifted towards greater revenue shares from consumption and labour taxes

The average tax revenue mix in the OECD is dominated by taxes on goods and services, social security contributions (SSCs) and personal income taxes (PIT) (Figure 2.17). Consumption taxes accounted for almost a third of total tax revenues on average in the OECD in 2013 while SSCs and PIT accounted respectively for 27% and 25% of total average tax revenues in the OECD. Corporate income taxes and property taxes, on the other hand, accounted for a comparatively small share of total average tax revenues (about 9% and 6% respectively).

Over time the average tax mix has shifted towards a greater share of revenues from taxes on consumption and labour income (Figure 2.17). Revenues as a share of GDP increased for all tax categories between 2010 and 2013 but the size of the revenue increase varied between taxes. Revenues from personal income taxes grew from 8.2% to 8.8% of

Figure 2.17. **Average tax mix in the OECD as a share of GDP**

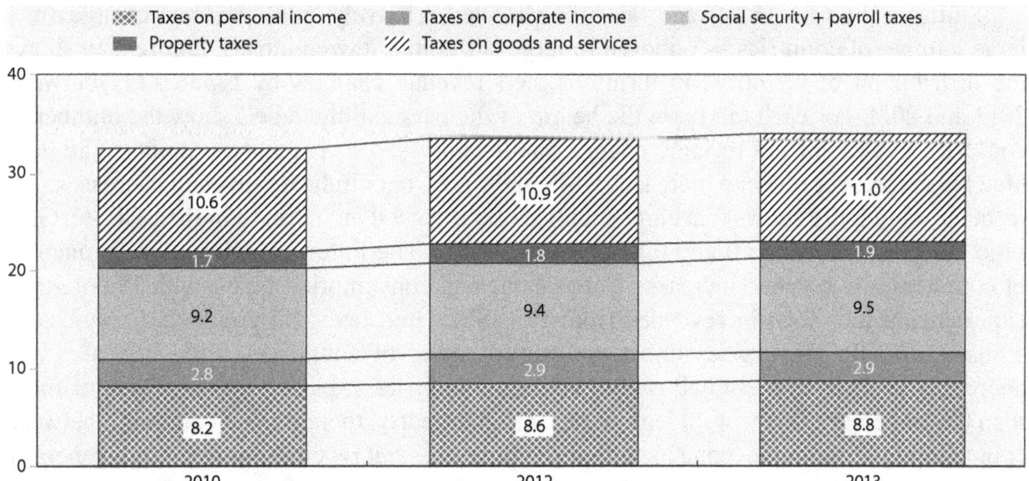

Source: OECD (2015), *Revenue Statistics 2015*, http://dx.doi.org/10.1787/rev_stats-2015-en-fr.

GDP and revenues from SSCs increased from 9.2% to 9.5% of GDP between 2010 and 2013. Over the same period, consumption tax revenues grew from 10.6% to 11% of GDP. Revenues from corporate taxes and property taxes, on the other hand, remained relatively stable between 2010 and 2013.

Tax mixes vary widely across countries. Figure 2.18 shows the main source of tax revenues in each country. Taxes on income and profits account for the largest source of tax revenues in 15 OECD countries. In Denmark, Australia and New Zealand, the share of taxes on income and profits account for more than half of total tax revenues. This is explained by the fact that New Zealand does not collect SSCs, that Australia only collects a small share of its revenues from payroll taxes and does not collect SSCs, and that the Danish Labour Market Contribution – which used to be considered as a SSC – was re-classified as PIT in 2008. In a number of other countries, including Central European and large Western European countries, SSCs are the primary source of tax revenues. Finally, some OECD countries, in particular emerging economies, collect most of their tax revenues from consumption taxes. VAT is also Hungary's primary source of tax revenues, in part because its VAT rate is the highest in the OECD.

Figure 2.18. **Main source of tax revenues by country as % of total tax revenues**

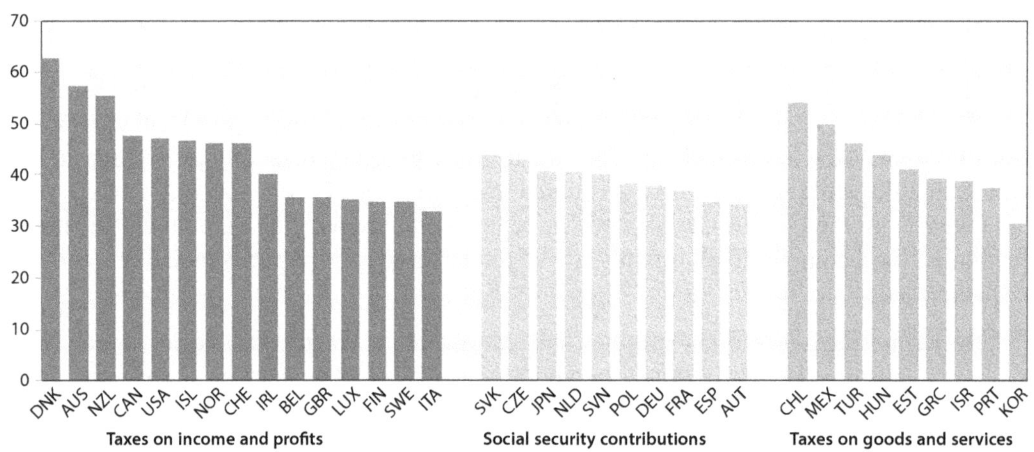

Source: OECD (2015), *Revenue Statistics 2015*, http://dx.doi.org/10.1787/rev_stats-2015-en-fr.

Shifts in the OECD average tax mix reflected relatively small revenue changes in a large number of countries as opposed to large shifts in a few countries. Figure 2.19 shows the distribution of countries in terms of their revenue changes by type of tax between 2013 and 2014. For each tax type, the height of the bars and the labels show the number of countries in each of the revenue change bands expressed in percentage points. The dark blue bars represent revenue increases while light grey bars indicate revenue decreases. For instance, the Figure shows that eight countries experienced an increase in their CIT-to-GDP ratio comprised between 0 and 0.1 percentage point. The Figure confirms that a majority of countries saw revenue increases from labour and consumption taxes, with 18 countries experiencing increases in revenues from PIT, SSCs and taxes on goods and services as a share of GDP. There was almost the same number of countries seeing increases and decreases in their CIT-to-GDP ratios, but nine countries experienced decreases of more than 0.2 percentage point. With regard to taxes on property, there was an equal split between countries experiencing revenue increases and decreases but revenue changes were generally minor.

Figure 2.19. **Revenue changes by type of tax between 2013 and 2014, distribution of countries**

Percentage point changes in tax-to-GDP ratios	PIT	CIT	SSCs	Property taxes	Taxes on goods and services
>1	1				1
0.5 to 1	1	1			2
0.2 to 0.5	6	2	5	1	6
0.1 to 0.2	4	2	6	4	3
0 to 0.1	6	8	7	10	6
-0.1 to 0	5	6	5	11	4
-0.2 to -0.1	4		3	3	6
-0.5 to -0.2	1	7	3		
-1 to -0.5		1		1	2
<-1		1			

Note: The total number of countries in each category of tax varies due to the absence of certain categories of taxes in certain countries and revenue data availability for 2014.

Source: OECD (2015), *Revenue Statistics 2015*, http://dx.doi.org/10.1787/rev_stats-2015-en-fr.

Notes

1. http://www.imf.org/external/np/speeches/2016/011216.htm.
2. http://www.skm.dk/english/facts-and-figures/the-tax-burden.

References

Brys, B., S. Perret, A. Thomas and P. O'Reilly (forthcoming, 2016), "Tax Design for Inclusive Economic Growth", *OECD Taxation Working Papers*, OECD Publishing, Paris.

Eyraud, L. and T. Wu (2015), "Playing by the rules: Reforming fiscal governance in Europe", *IMF Working Papers*, No. 15/67, International Monetary Fund, Washington DC.

IMF (2015), *World Economic Outlook*, April 2015.

OECD (2016a), *OECD Global Interim Economic Outlook*, February 2016, http://dx.doi.org/10.1787/eco_outlook-v2015-sup2-en.

OECD (2016b), "Income distribution", *OECD Social and Welfare Statistics* (database), http://dx.doi.org/10.1787/data-00654-en.

OECD. (2015a), "OECD Economic Outlook No. 98 (Edition 2015/2)", *OECD Economic Outlook: Statistics and Projections* (database), http://dx.doi.org/10.1787/bd810434-en.

OECD (2015b), *OECD Employment Outlook 2015*, OECD Publishing, Paris, http://dx.doi.org/10.1787/empl_outlook-2015-en.

OECD (2015c), *In It Together: Why Less Inequality Benefits All*, OECD Publishing, Paris, http://dx.doi.org/10.1787/9789264235120-en.

OECD (2015d) "FDI in Figures", October 2015, http://www.oecd.org/investment/FDI-in-Figures-October-2015.pdf.

OECD (2015e), *The Future of Productivity*, OECD Publishing, Paris, http://dx.doi.org/10.1787/9789264248533-en.

OECD (2015f), *Revenue Statistics 2015*, OECD Publishing, Paris, http://dx.doi.org/10.1787/rev_stats-2015-en-fr.

UNCTAD (2015), *World Investment Report 2015: Reforming International Investment Governance*, United Nations Publication, Geneva.

Chapter 3

Tax policy developments in 2015

This chapter provides an overview of the tax reforms that were introduced in 2015 in OECD countries. It identifies the most significant reforms that were implemented, enacted or announced in calendar year 2015 as well as common tax policy trends across groups of countries. It starts with a general overview of tax reforms across OECD countries and their estimated revenue effects. It then looks at each category of tax separately including personal income taxes and social security contributions, corporate income taxes and other corporate taxes, VAT/GST and excise duties, environmentally related taxes and property taxes. This chapter aims to inform tax policy discussions as well as to support member and non-member countries in their assessment and design of future tax reforms.

The statistical data for Israel are supplied by and under the responsibility of the relevant Israeli authorities. The use of such data by the OECD is without prejudice to the status of the Golan Heights, East Jerusalem and Israeli settlements in the West Bank under the terms of international law.

Austria, Belgium, Greece, Japan, the Netherlands, Norway and Spain were identified as the countries that implemented, legislated or announced the most comprehensive tax reforms in 2015. In Austria, Belgium and the Netherlands, the main objective was to reduce taxes on labour income with a view to encouraging employment and increasing households' disposable incomes. In Norway and Japan, a key consideration was to support investment through a reduction of taxes on corporate income. Spain's tax reform involved both corporate and labour tax cuts to boost the economy. Finally, Greece introduced significant reforms, in particular in the areas of VAT and CIT, to respond to the demands of the European Commission, the European Central Bank and the International Monetary Fund.

However, not all of these comprehensive tax reforms appeared to be revenue neutral, raising some concerns about their sustainability. In some countries, the reforms aimed at lowering taxes on labour or corporate income involved (partial) shifts towards increased consumption taxes (Austria, Belgium, Norway), but not in all. Besides, in the countries where there were shifts towards consumption taxes, these were not necessarily significant enough to compensate for the revenue losses from cuts in direct taxes.

Across all OECD countries, many of the reforms focused on reducing taxes on labour and corporate income. Table 3.1 summarises the revenue effects of the tax policy measures that were reported in the 2016 Annual Tax Policy Reform Questionnaire based on revenue estimates provided by WP2 Delegates. These measures include (1) the reforms that entered into force in 2015; (2) the reforms that were legislated in 2015, which for the most part entered into force in January 2016; and (3) the reforms that were announced in 2015 which will be effective in 2016 or later. This table is not intended to provide a precise estimation of the revenue effects of reforms but gives an idea of broad tax revenue shifts in OECD countries. The table suggests that reforms were often aimed at lowering corporate and labour taxes, with partial revenue increases in or shifts towards consumption and environmentally related taxes. There were only a limited number of reforms in the area of property taxes.

Table 3.1. **Estimated revenue effects of the tax reforms implemented, legislated and announced in 2015**

Revenue decrease		Revenue increase
AUT, BEL, CZE, DEU, ESP, EST, HUN, IRL, ISL, MEX, NLD, NOR, SVK, TUR, USA	**Personal income taxes**	AUS, CHE, SWE
BEL, CHE, EST, HUN, ITA, SVK, USA	**SSCs and payroll taxes**	ISR, LUX, SWE
AUS, CAN, ESP, EST, FRA, IRL, ISR, ITA, NLD, NOR, POL, SVN, TUR, USA	**Corporate income taxes**	AUT, BEL, CHL, GBR, GRC, HUN, KOR
CZE, HUN, ISL, ISR, SVK, TUR	**Value-added tax**	AUS, AUT, BEL, EST, LUX, GRC, NOR, NZL, POL, SVN, SWE
ISL	**Non-energy Excise duties**	BEL, CZE, EST, GRC, HUN, IRL, LUX, NLD, NZL, NOR, PRT, SVK, SWE, TUR
DNK	**Environmentally related taxes**	BEL, EST, FRA, FIN, GBR, NLD, NZL, PRT, SWE
GBR, IRL, ITA, NLD, NOR	**Property taxes**	AUT, FIN, ISR

Source: OECD Annual Tax Policy Reform Questionnaire.

3.1. Personal income tax and social security contributions

This section shows that after several years of steady increases, the OECD average tax burden on labour income stabilised in 2015. However, reforms that were announced and legislated in 2015, which will generally become effective in 2016, seem to point to a trend of declining tax burdens on labour income. There were some decreases in PIT rates levied on labour income combined with an expansion of allowances and credits, targeted in particular at low-income taxpayers and households with children. With respect to the taxation of personal capital income, several countries increased tax rates on dividends and other sources of capital income, while others provided targeted provisions to encourage pension savings and employee share purchases.

After several years of steady increases, taxes on labour income stabilised in 2015

In the years following the crisis, there were steady increases in the OECD average tax burden on labour income, though it did not return to the levels seen before the crisis. In the years leading up to the crisis, the tax burden on labour income decreased substantially (see Figure 3.1). These reductions were particularly concentrated on families with children. In the post-crisis period, tax rates rose broadly on all family types, with a particular concentration on one-earner married couples with children. However, even though these average rates have risen over the past eight years, tax rates are still below where they were 15 years ago. These rises are potentially problematic given the high unemployment rates across the OECD (see Chapter 2, Figure 2.7).

Figure 3.1. **Changes to labour income tax wedges by family type**

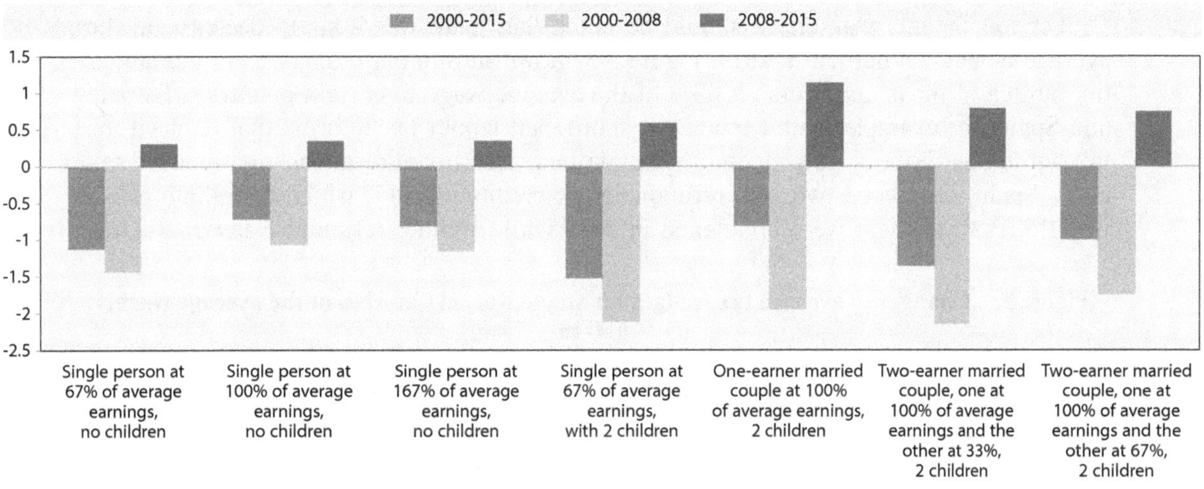

Source: OECD Taxing Wages Database, http://dx.doi.org/10.1787/data-00265-en.

The higher labour tax burden in the post-crisis period resulted in an increase in revenues. These increases have been driven largely by taxes on individuals' income and profits, and by modest increases in employees' SSCs. Figure 3.2 shows modest rises in revenues from income taxes overall, with taxes on individuals' income and profits increasing from 10.9% of GDP in 2010 to 11.5% in 2013. The whole of this increase was accounted for personal income taxes with corporate income taxes as a share of GDP remaining unchanged. Similarly, with respect to SSCs, employee's SSCs have increased modestly (from 3.1% of GDP in 2010 to 3.3% in 2013) while tax receipts from employer's SSCs have remained relatively flat (from 5.15% in 2010 to 5.2% in 2013).

Figure 3.2. **PIT and SSCs in the tax mix**

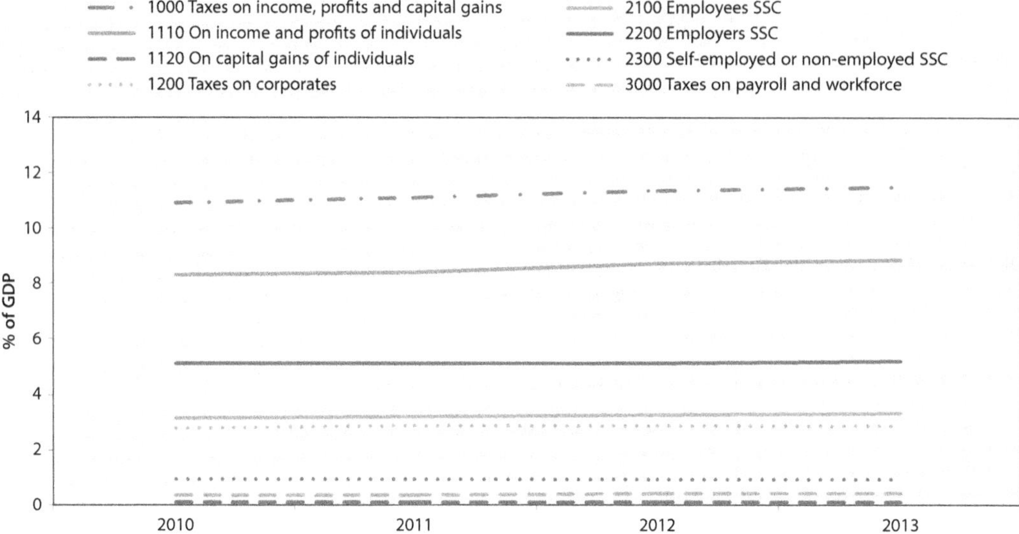

Source: OECD (2015), *Revenue Statistics 2015*, http://dx.doi.org/10.1787/rev_stats-2015-en-fr.

In 2015, however, the OECD average tax burden on labour income stabilised. According to the latest *Taxing Wages* report, the tax wedge on labour income for the average worker across the OECD stabilised at 35.9% in 2015. While taxes on labour income increased by relatively small amounts in 24 out of the 34 OECD countries, this was offset by decreases in eight countries in 2015. Estonia, Greece and Spain experienced significant decreases of at least one percentage point (OECD, 2016a).

For low-income workers, it should be noted that there was a slight decrease in the average labour tax burden in 2015. Figure 3.3 shows substantial reductions in the labour tax burden of those taxpayers on 67% of the average wage in certain countries. Estonia and Spain, for example, both carried out significant labour tax reforms that reduced the tax burden on those on low incomes. Estonia increased tax allowances, and reduced tax rates. Spain introduced two new refundable tax credits in 2014, which came into effect in 2015. Both of them were broadened in 2015 while another refundable tax credit was

Figure 3.3. **Changes to average tax wedges for single workers at 67% of the average wage, 2014-15**

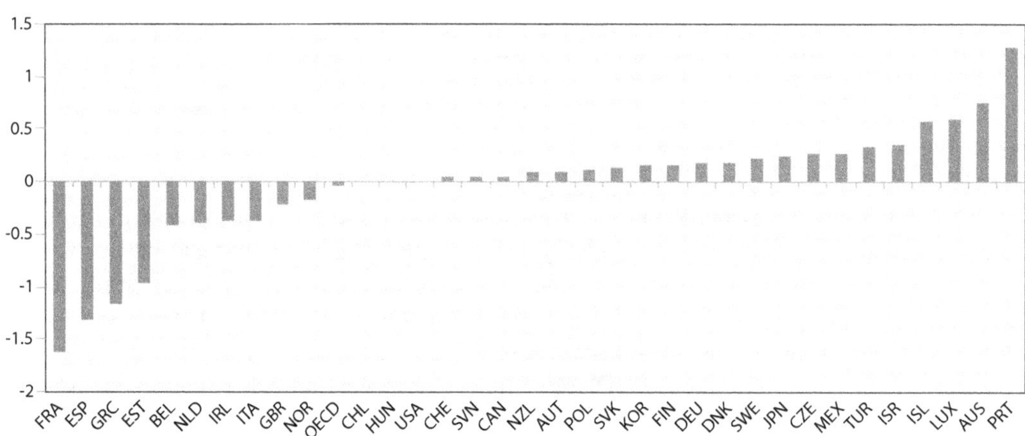

Source: OECD Taxing Wages Database, http://dx.doi.org/10.1787/data-00265-en.

also introduced and came into force in 2015. Spain also increased family allowances and reduced rates in all brackets. The overall decrease in the tax burden on low-income workers for the OECD on average was small, however, because of tax burden increases in a number of other countries. Tax burden increases on low-income workers were particularly high in Portugal where the system of tax credits was made less progressive and in Luxembourg which implemented a general rate increase.

Tax levels on labour income are likely to decline in 2016

The reforms that were announced and legislated in 2015, which will generally become effective in 2016, seem to point to a trend of declining tax burdens on labour income. There were some decreases in PIT rates levied on labour income in OECD countries combined with an expansion of allowances and credits. Nine countries have reduced various income tax rates, with these rate reductions being concentrated on those on lower incomes (see Table 3.2 and Annex A for further details). Rate reductions have been accompanied by base broadening in some of these countries, though not in all. In some countries, including Belgium, Austria and the Netherlands, these reforms were part of a more comprehensive effort to shift tax burdens away from labour income (see Box 3.1). This pattern has not been uniform, however, a smaller number of countries have taken steps to increase the tax burden on labour income, in particular through base broadening (noticeably Sweden, which carried out a large tax reform this year).

Table 3.2. **Summary of changes to labour income tax legislated or announced in 2015**

	Rate reduction/Base narrowed	Rate increase/Base broadening
Top rate	BEL, ESP, EST, HUN	AUT
Non-top rate	AUT, BEL, ESP, EST, FRA, ISL, IRL, NLD, NOR	
Personal allowances, credits, tax brackets	FIN, DEU, ESP, MEX, SVN	NLD, SWE
Targeted low income/EITCs	AUT, BEL, ESP, FRA, NLD, SVK, SWE, USA	AUS
Children & other dependents	AUT, CZE, DEU, IRL, NLD, TUR, USA	EST
Elderly & disabled	NLD, SWE	
Miscellaneous expenses & deductions	BEL	AUT, SWE, CHE
Education	TUR, USA	EST, SWE

Note: Provisions legislated or announced before 2015 that take effect in 2015 are omitted from this table.
Source: OECD Annual Tax Policy Reform Questionnaire.

Box 3.1. **The Belgian tax mix reform**

In December 2015, Belgium enacted a comprehensive tax reform. The reform was designed to boost employment, competitiveness, and disposable income for low and middle-income earners. The tax burden shifted away from labour and towards other tax bases. The reform is consistent with the advice that Belgium has been receiving from many international institutions, including the OECD: shift taxes (including SSCs) partially away from labour.

Box 3.1. **The Belgian tax mix reform** *(continued)*

The main provisions that were agreed upon by the government include:

Cuts to PIT and SSCs:

- The nominal employer SSC rate decreased, with the reductions targeted at low-income earners,
- The standard deduction for professional expenses increased, with improved targeting at low-income earners,
- The zero-rate PIT band increased,
- Marginal tax rates fell.

These cuts were funded through:

- Measures against tax fraud,
- An increase in excise duties on diesel, tobacco and alcoholic drinks,
- A health tax on sodas and other high-sugar content products,
- An increase in the taxation of savings,
- An increase in VAT on electricity from the reduced to the standard rate.

Estimations show that low and middle-income earners will experience the largest drop in average income tax rates (over 5 percentage points). The largest part of this reduction will come from the increase in the allowance for work-related expenses. So those on lower incomes will see their purchasing power rise, with possible improvements to work incentives, while labour demand will increase as a result of the reduction in employer SSCs.

Changes to marginal tax rates are comparatively minor, but the responsiveness of working hours to tax rate changes tends to be relatively low compared to the responsiveness of labour market participation. Therefore, modest reductions in marginal tax rates may be warranted.

The reform will increase tax progressivity, but the redistributive effect of taxation will be lower because of the reduction in the average income tax rate. While the reform should improve employment opportunities, work incentives and the purchasing power especially of lower incomes, some uncertainty remains with respect to the overall budgetary impact of the reform.

Some countries have reduced their top PIT rate on labour income, though these reductions have been modest. Overall, top PIT rates in the OECD in 2015 are below what they were in 2000 (see Figure 3.4). However, this reflects large reductions in top PIT rates in the period leading up to the financial crisis. Rates rose in the years following the crisis, though not to levels seen in 2000. In 2015, these rates were reduced in some countries, but only modestly. Belgium reduced its 45% top rate, Estonia reduced the rate from 21% to 20%, and Hungary reduced its general rate from 16% to 15%. Several countries have reduced tax rates below the top statutory rate. Belgium, Estonia, France, Iceland, Ireland, the Netherlands and Norway all carried out rate-reducing reforms. Austria reduced its minimum PIT rate but raised its top tax rate from 50% to 55%.

The PIT base has generally been narrowed as a result of the reform legislated or announced in 2015. There has been an expansion of PIT allowances and credits (see Table 3.2). Finland, Germany and Mexico all narrowed their tax bases through expansions of allowances or shifts in tax brackets. However, the Netherlands and Sweden – both of which engaged in substantial tax reforms – expanded their tax base. The Netherlands decreased their general tax credit, though they expanded their earned income credit. Sweden broadened their tax base by reducing or eliminating tax expenditures for household work, administrative expenses, charitable donations, and building repairs and maintenance.

Figure 3.4. **Top statutory PIT rates in 2000 and 2015**

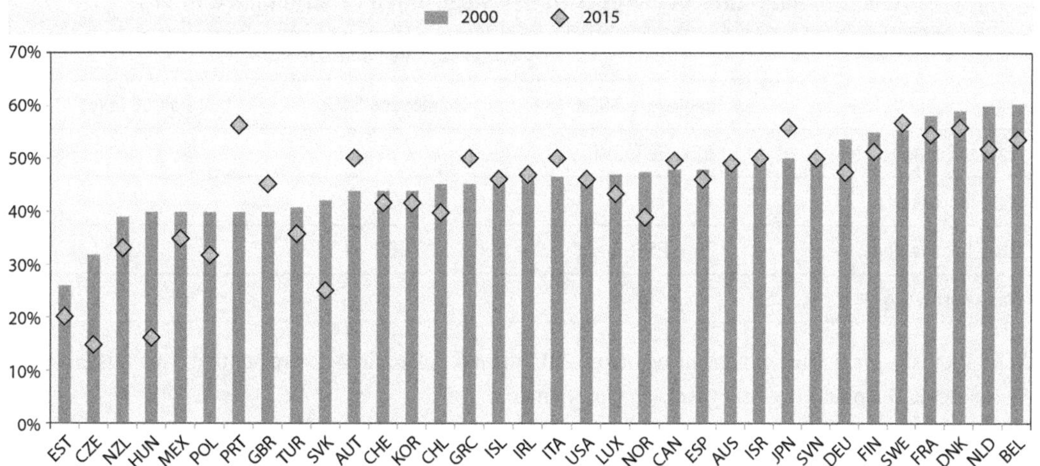

Source: OECD Tax Database, www.oecd.org/tax/tax-policy/tax-database.htm.

Some of the expansion in allowances and credits has been aimed at low-income workers. Seven countries expanded provisions aimed at low-income workers. In particular, the Netherlands, Sweden and the United States expanded earned income tax credits, continuing the increased use of these kinds of credits in OECD countries (OECD, 2011). Belgium legislated an increase in the "work bonus" in 2016. Austria expanded its non-wastable tax credits for low-income earners. Figure 3.3 shows that, while some countries have reduced the tax wedge on low-income workers in 2014, most countries have actually increased the tax burden on these taxpayers. Thus the trends with respect to low-income taxpayers are mixed – some increases in the tax burden have been accompanied by expansions in provisions aimed at encouraging work.

There has also been an expansion of provisions aimed at families with children. Seven countries expanded their provisions aimed at households with children and other dependents (see Table 3.2). This stands in contrast to the broader trends in the post-crisis period, where households with children saw their income tax burdens rise more than families without children (see Figure 3.1). Austria doubled its tax allowance for children; the Czech Republic increased its tax credit for second and other children in 2015 and announced a further increase for 2016 and 2017; Turkey doubled the allowance for children after the third child. The Netherlands increased their tax credit for combining work and childcare, while the United States made permanent a reduction in the earnings threshold for the refundable portion of the child tax credit.

Measures legislated and announced in 2015 also reduced the tax burden on low-income workers through reduced SSCs. The SSC burden has broadly fallen – due to legislated or announced rate reductions in some countries, and due to base narrowing. This has largely been targeted at low-income workers (see Table 3.2). These may have positive effects on both inequality and employment rates for low-income workers (see Chapter 2). As was the case in 2014, however, this pattern was by no means uniform. Three countries, Germany,

Israel and Sweden, raised SSCs or payroll taxes in 2015 (see Table 3.3), while Spain broadened the SSC base and the United States expanded the payroll tax base. So while some countries attempt to reduce rates or target rate reductions at low-income workers to reduce labour supply, other countries, particularly those whose economies grew strongly in 2015, were able to carry out countercyclical policies, raising revenue by increasing taxation of labour supply.

Table 3.3. **Summary of changes to SSCs legislated or announced in 2015**

	Social security contributions		
	Employers SSCs	**Employees SSCs**	**Payroll taxes**
Rate reduction	BEL, EST, CHE	CHE	
Rate increase	ISR	DEU	SWE
Base broadening	ESP	ESP	USA
Base narrowing	ITA		

Note: Provisions legislated or announced before 2015 that take effect in 2015 are omitted from this table.

Source: OECD Annual Tax Policy Reform Questionnaire.

Several countries increased tax rates on dividends and other types of capital income

With respect to the taxation of capital income, several countries have increased tax rates on dividends and other sources of capital income, including Belgium, Finland, Norway, and Sweden. Belgium introduced a capital gains tax on speculative capital gains (gains on listed stocks held for less than six months). Austria raised tax rates on capital gains, while Ireland reduced them (see Table 3.4). Several other countries have narrowed the tax base with respect to capital income, making special provisions for pension contributions (such as Mexico) or for employee share acquisitions (such as Australia and Austria). Only Sweden undertook base-broadening reforms with respect to capital taxes over the last year. Finally, the Netherlands legislated a budget-neutral capital income tax reform.

Table 3.4. **Summary of changes to the taxation of savings legislated or announced in 2015**

	Dividend and interest income	**Capital gains**	**Rental income**	**Pension contributions***	**Charitable giving deductions**	**Employee share acquisition deductions**
Rate reduction		IRL				
Rate increase	BEL, FIN, NOR, SWE	AUT, BEL, FIN	FIN			
Base broadening	SWE				SWE	
Base narrowed		SVK	EST, ISL	MEX		AUS, AUT

Note: Provisions legislated or announced before 2015 that take effect in 2015 are omitted from this table.

* This column does not include changes in the taxation of pension income, only changes in taxation of pension contributions.

Source: OECD Annual Tax Policy Reform Questionnaire.

The tax rate increases on dividend income introduced in several countries seem to follow a broader post-crisis pattern. The overall tax burden on dividend income is a combination of the taxation of profits at the corporate level with taxes at the personal shareholder level. These may include income taxes, withholding taxes, and taxes on presumptive rates of return (Harding, 2013). Figure 3.5 shows that the total tax burden on dividend income has increased slightly since the crisis, in contrast with the pre-crisis period during which the tax burden on dividend income generally decreased. The post-crisis rise in dividend taxation has been the result of increased taxation at the shareholder level while corporate tax rates continued to decrease modestly. Nevertheless, there were still wide differences in the ways OECD countries taxed dividends in 2015 (Figure 3.6).

Figure 3.5. **Changes in top tax rates on dividends and top labour incomes**

Combined statutory tax rate on dividends
Top personal tax wedges
Top personal tax rates
Corporate income tax rate
60
50
40
30
20
10
0
46.4
43.1
42.0
25.0
2000 2001 2002 2003 2004 2005 2006 2007 2008 2009 2010 2011 2012 2013 2014 2015

Note: The top personal tax wedge is the marginal tax wedge at the income level where the top statutory PIT rate first applies. The results take into account basic/standard income tax allowances and tax credits. The reported marginal tax rate may not be the maximum possible marginal tax rate. A higher rate may be observed for higher income earners where tax allowance provisions may be diminished or eliminated. A higher rate may also be possible at lower levels of income where there is a withdrawal of a tax relief.

Source: OECD Tax Database, www.oecd.org/tax/tax-policy/tax-database.htm.

Figure 3.6. **Combined top statutory tax rates on dividend income, 2015**

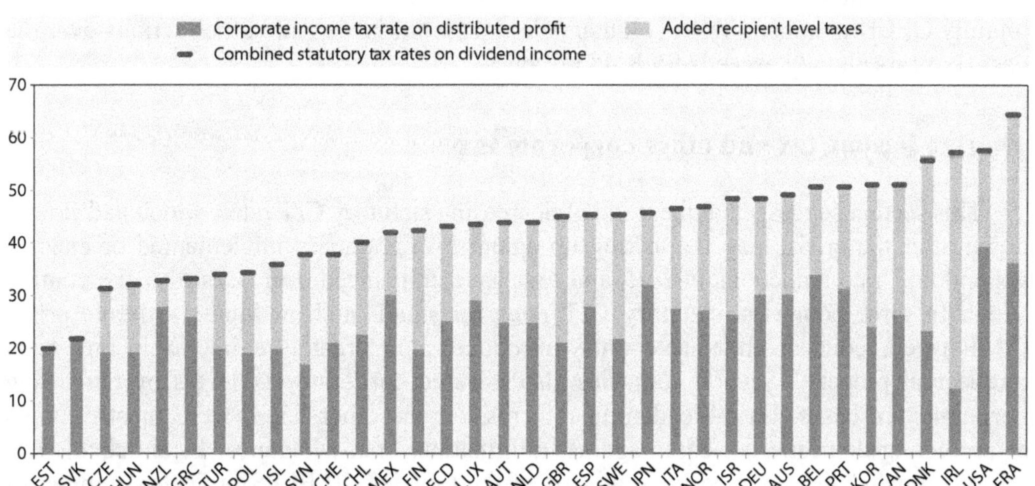

Source: OECD Tax Database, www.oecd.org/tax/tax-policy/tax-database.htm.

Overall, there remains a gap in OECD countries between tax rates on dividends and tax rates on labour income. When taking both taxes at the corporate level and the individual level into account, Figure 3.5 shows that the taxation of dividends is above the top marginal PIT rate. However, labour income is also subject to SSCs and payroll taxes, which are not usually levied on dividend income. Incorporating SSCs and payroll taxes, the total top marginal tax wedge on labour income is greater than the combined statutory tax rates faced on dividend income. In 2015, the average combined statutory tax rate on dividends was 43.1%, compared to a top statutory tax wedge of 46.4% on labour income. This gap therefore suggests that workers may have incentives to re-characterise labour income as capital income in the OECD. Of course, there are many other different forms of capital income, many of which are taxed differently. In particular, dividends are taxed in many countries at higher rates than interest, capital gains, private pension savings and immovable property.

The increase in statutory tax rates on dividends, both since the crisis and over the last year, could be a response to a renewed focus on inequality between labour and capital in recent years, and a renewed emphasis on the need for tax design to promote inclusive growth (Brys et al., forthcoming). These increases could also be due to a potentially reduced ease of tax evasion with respect to capital income in recent years. Importantly, Kopczuk (2005) and others have shown that base broadening can lower the efficiency costs of higher taxes on capital income by reducing opportunities for tax avoidance and the negative distortions that arise from them.

In this context, a key tax policy development in 2015 was the approval by the OECD Council in July 2015 of the Common Reporting Standard (CRS) on the Automatic Exchange of Information for Tax Purposes. This Standard calls on jurisdictions to obtain information from their financial institutions and automatically exchange that information with other jurisdictions on an annual basis. Ratings are given to countries under the peer review process of the exchange of information on request, which is carried out by the Global Forum on Transparency and Exchange of Information. Almost all OECD countries were given a rating of "Compliant" or "Largely Compliant". In addition, almost all OECD countries will engage in automatic exchange of financial account information in tax matters by 2018. This increased transparency is expected to result in reduced personal capital income tax evasion in Global Forum member countries in the future. The political agreement to adopt the Standard has already had a positive impact on the yield drawn from voluntary disclosure programmes, as shown for example by the successful programmes recently launched by France and Italy. Additional revenue identified in 30 countries (mainly OECD members) from voluntary disclosure initiatives and other actions over the past six years already exceeds EUR 48 billion.

3.2. Corporate income tax and other corporate taxes

This section suggests that the trend of decreasing statutory CIT rates, which had slowed down after the crisis, may be picking up again. Five countries implemented or enacted general CIT rate reductions in 2015 and four have announced decreases over the coming years. In three countries, statutory CIT rates for small- and medium-sized enterprises (SMEs) were reduced, while one country introduced a preferential regime for income from intellectual property. Several countries also lowered corporate tax levels by narrowing corporate tax bases. Base-broadening reforms, on the other hand, were mostly aimed at protecting domestic tax bases against multinational tax avoidance. In anticipation of the recommendations agreed upon as part of the OECD/G20 BEPS project, a number of countries enacted specific anti-avoidance legislation.

The trend of corporate tax rate reductions, which had slowed down after the crisis, seems to be gaining renewed momentum

The trend of decreasing top statutory CIT rates slowed down after the crisis. The average combined (i.e. national and local) corporate tax rate across OECD countries has been declining over the last 20 years (Figure 3.7). Starting from a level of above 32% in 2000, the OECD unweighted average decreased in the following eight years by about 0.83 percentage points annually, reaching 26% in 2008 and 25% in 2015. Although successive reductions continued after the crisis, the average annual decrease was much lower, 0.14 percentage points, in the period 2009-15. The largest decreases over the entire period have been experienced in Germany (21.9 pp.), Canada (16.1 pp.), Greece (14 pp.) and Turkey (13 pp.). Only two countries – Hungary and Chile – raised their rates, by one and 7.5 percentage points respectively. Nevertheless, with the exception of the strong reduction in the German rate in 2001, the range between the highest and the lowest statutory CIT rates has remained fairly stable.

Figure 3.7. **Combined statutory CIT rates, in %, by country**

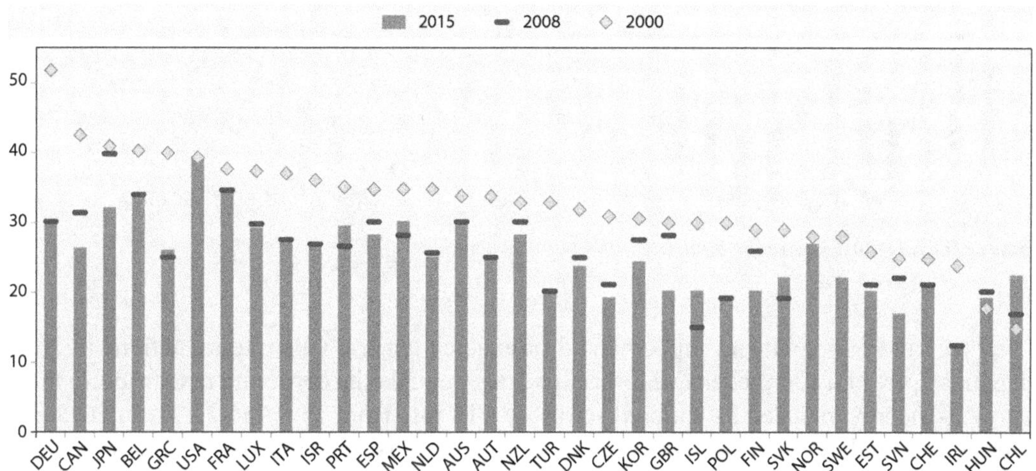

Source: OECD Tax Database, www.oecd.org/tax/tax-policy/tax-database.htm.

After the crisis, CIT revenues as a share of GDP decreased in most countries (Figure 3.8). While there is considerable variation across OECD countries, CIT revenues as a share of GDP amounted to around 3.3% on average in 2000. In the years preceding the crisis this share increased in most countries, culminating at an average share of 3.6% in 2007. However, in the years following the crisis, all but eight countries – New Zealand, Japan, Israel, Denmark, Iceland, Estonia, Turkey and the United States – experienced a decrease in the share of CIT revenues to GDP. In some countries, notably Greece and Spain, this development may have been driven mainly by poor economic performance in the post-crisis years. In other countries, such as Australia, Norway, Finland, Netherlands and the United Kingdom, relative decreases in CIT revenues coincide with solid economic performance.

Recent tax policy changes with reported revenue effects are expected to reduce CIT revenues in the majority of OECD countries. 22 countries reported the enactment or implementation of a total of 59 corporate tax measures in 2015. Revenue estimates provided by WP2 Delegates show that out of this total, 30 measures (i.e. more than half) are expected to reduce tax revenues, whereas 22 are expected to have a revenue raising effect, five a neutral effect and the other two uncertain effects on revenues. On the whole, positive revenue effects are expected to prevail in only seven out of the 22 countries, while negative effects are likely to dominate in 13 countries. However, many countries do not report revenue effects of legislative changes that protect the tax base. Further, many of the BEPS Project's changes can be implemented through regulatory measures (e.g. increased transparency with country-by-country reporting, implementation of the revised OECD transfer pricing guidelines) which generally are not estimated for their revenue effects.

Figure 3.8. **CIT revenues, in % of GDP, by country**

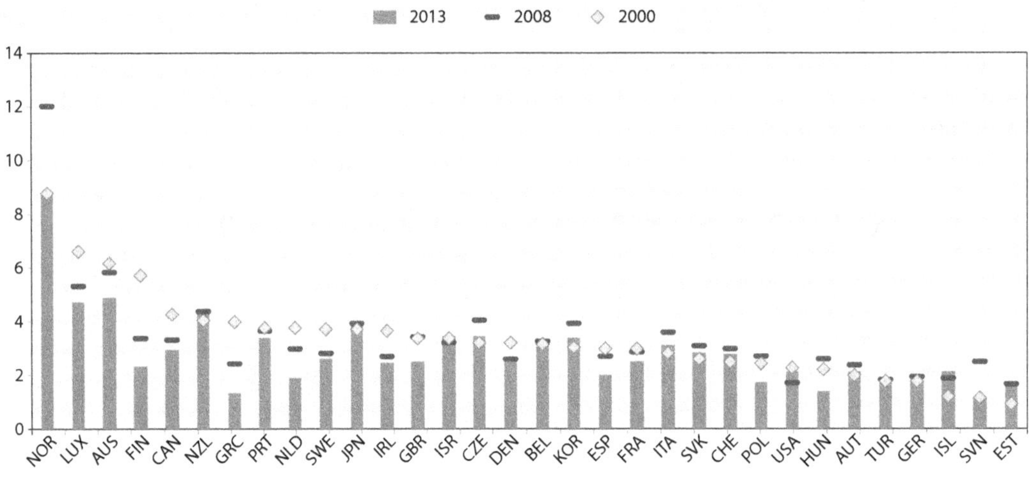

2013 | 2008 | 2000

NOR LUX AUS FIN CAN NZL GRC PRT NLD SWE JPN IRL GBR ISR CZE DEN BEL KOR ESP FRA ITA SVK CHE POL USA HUN AUT TUR GER ISL SVN EST

Source: OECD (2015), *Revenue Statistics 2015*, http://dx.doi.org/10.1787/rev_stats-2015-en-fr.

Five out of 34 countries implemented or enacted general CIT rate reductions in 2015. Japan, as part of a comprehensive reform package to make its corporate tax structure more growth-friendly, reduced its national statutory CIT rate from 25.5% to 23.9% in 2015 (see Box 3.2). Standard local enterprise taxes rates were also lowered from 7.2% to 6% and further to 4.8%. Taken together, these changes lower the combined national and local tax rate from 34.6% (before 2015) to 32.1% in the fiscal year 2015. As part of a comprehensive tax reform as well, Spain lowered its CIT rate from 30% to 28% in 2015 and to 25% in 2016. Norway introduced a 2 percentage point CIT rate decrease, taking effect in January 2016. Israel enacted a reduction of 1.5 percentage points which took effect at the same time. A smaller decrease of 1 percentage point was enacted in Estonia. Greece was the only country to raise its national statutory CIT rate, from 26% to 29% in 2015. In Canada, the province of Alberta increased its local corporate income tax rate by two percentage points.

Box 3.2. **Japan's comprehensive corporate tax reform**

At the end of 2014, Japan announced a comprehensive reform package aimed at making its corporate tax system more growth-friendly. It consists of several components which started to take effect in 2015.

Box 3.2. **Japan's comprehensive corporate tax reform** *(continued)*

First, the national statutory CIT rate was reduced from 25.5% to 23.9% in 2015. Second, standard local enterprise taxes rates were also lowered from 7.2% to 6% and further to 4.8%. Taken together, these changes lower the combined national and local tax rate from 34.6% (before 2015) to 32.1% in the fiscal year 2015.

In March 2016, further reductions were legislated, successively reducing the national rate to 23.4% (2016 and 2017) and 23.2% (2018), while the local enterprise tax is reduced to 3.6%. These scheduled reductions will bring down the combined rate to below 30% over the next two years.

In addition, the reform package contained several base broadening measures including a simplification of the tax depreciation system, a reduction in the maximum amount of net operating loss deductions that can be carried forward for tax purposes as well as the reduction and elimination of several special tax concessions. Additional positive revenue effects are expected from a gradual shift in the tax base of the local enterprise tax.

Australia, Spain and Canada also lowered CIT rates for SMEs. Australia reduced its CIT rate by 1.5 percentage points for smaller incorporated businesses on the basis of a turnover threshold to improve their cash flow and encourage growth. In Spain, companies with a turnover under EUR 10 million benefitted from a reduced rate of 25% applied to the first EUR 300 000 of taxable income and a 28% rate to the excess in 2015. This reduced rate no longer applies as the standard rate is now 25%. In Canada, the federal small business tax rate was reduced from 11% in 2015 to 10.5% in 2016. While further rate reductions were legislated to reduce the rate gradually to 9% in 2019, the government announced in March 2016 that further rate reductions below 10.5% have been deferred and legislation has been introduced that has the effect of cancelling the reductions for 2017, 2018 and 2019.

The revenue impacts from CIT rate reductions are expected to range between 0.1 and 0.5% of current GDP over the next four years. The revenue decreases from each of these reforms are expected to be highest in Estonia, 0.5% of current GDP over the next four years, Israel, 0.4% over four years, and Norway, 0.2% only in the first year after the reform. Relative revenue impacts in other countries are expected to be somewhat lower, ranging from around 0.2% to below 0.1% over four years. In Spain, the overall impact of the complete CIT reform package, including the rate reduction as well as other base reforms, is currently estimated to be around -0.3% of GDP in 2015 and 2016.

In addition, the United Kingdom, France, Japan and Italy have announced CIT rate cuts in the coming years. The United Kingdom committed to a gradual decrease in its statutory CIT rate from 20% to 19% in 2017 and 17% in 2020. As part of a comprehensive reform package (i.e. *Pacte de responsabilité et de solidarité*), France announced a decrease in its statutory CIT rate from 34.4% to 28% by 2020 but did not provide a detailed schedule for rate reductions. The 10.7% exceptional surcharge on corporate income tax liability, which has been effective since 2012, will also expire at the end of 2016. Japan announced further CIT rate cuts, successively reducing the national rate to 23.4% (2016 and 2017) and 23.2% (2018), while the local enterprise tax will be lowered to 3.6%. These scheduled reductions will bring down the combined rate to below 30% over the next two years. In Italy, the 2016 Stability Law approved a CIT rate decrease from 27.5% to 24% as from 2017.

Ireland introduced a Knowledge Development Box which offers a reduced CIT rate for certain income from intellectual property (IP). The Irish Knowledge Development Box, which became effective on 1 January 2016, grants a tax rate of 6.25% (compared to the statutory rate of 12.5%) on the share of profits corresponding to the proportion of qualifying research and development (R&D) expenditures in Ireland compared to the total R&D expenditures incurred in the development of the IP asset. Qualifying intangibles are patents and copyrighted software. This Knowledge Development Box is in line with the OECD nexus approach, which is built upon substantial activity requirements, using qualified R&D expenditures as a proxy for research activity. It ensures that tax benefits are granted only to the extent to which the income-generating activities required to produce the IP are actually carried out in Ireland.

Several countries narrowed their corporate tax bases to support R&D, SMEs and investment

Some countries introduced more targeted tax relief for innovation-related income. Poland introduced tax exemptions for capital gains from venture capital and revenues from the commercialisation of intellectual property by qualified taxpayers, such as educational and research institutions. Both income-based measures will expire at the end of 2017. Turkey enacted a new law which provides tax benefits for donations to a specific science support foundation.

R&D tax incentives remained an important policy instrument to encourage innovation. In 2015, existing indirect R&D support schemes were expanded in Austria, Poland, Turkey and the United States. Austria increased its volume-based tax credit from 10% to 12%, reducing corporate tax revenues by around EUR 320 million over four years. Poland introduced a new tax relief, which contains an additional deduction from the tax base for a proportion of qualifying expenses incurred on R&D activities. This relief became effective in 2016 and replaced the previous relief for the acquisition of new technologies. In total, the innovation related tax reforms in Poland are expected to reduce tax revenues by around EUR 185 million over four years. In December 2015, the United States permanently extended its research and experimentation tax credit. Previously, the credit had only been extended on a temporary basis; this measure is therefore expected to encourage long-term commitment to research activities in the private sector. The tax credit was also enhanced to allow SMEs and start-ups to claim tax relief against alternative minimum or payroll tax liabilities. The revenue cost of this measure is estimated to be around USD 30.6 billion over four years.

Turkey introduced an allowance for corporate equity (ACE) for newly issued equity. The ACE equals 50 per cent of the imputed return on the newly issued equity as from 1 July 2015 onwards, thereby significantly lowering the marginal corporate effective tax rate on investment financed with newly issued equity (the ACE does not apply to retained profits). The imputed return equals the annual weighted average interest rate applied to Turkish-denominated loans provided by banks. The ACE does not apply to the financial, banking and insurance sectors. Holdings and other corporations that earn a significant share of passive income are excluded as well. A number of base protection measures have been implemented in order to ensure that the ACE applies only to new equity-financed investment.

Some countries narrowed their corporate income tax bases through enhanced or accelerated tax depreciation allowances, also contributing to a reduction in the corporate tax burden. Italy introduced a temporary provision which grants 40% enhanced depreciation for new investments in plants, machinery and buildings until the end of 2016. Spain enacted a comprehensive restructuring of its depreciation system; measures include a simplification of depreciation rates, unlimited loss carry-forwards as well as the abolishment of the upper limit on depreciation. The United States permanently extended the increased expensing provision for SMEs and bonus depreciation was also modified and extended.

Reductions in the corporate tax burden are aimed at encouraging investment and increasing international competitiveness. As discussed in Chapter 2, the recovery in business investment between 2011 and 2015, measured by the annual change in private non-residential gross fixed capital formation, has been limited in scope and uneven across countries. Given this macroeconomic background, the main policy objective of the measures discussed in this section so far, i.e. general or targeted rate reductions and base narrowing, has been to encourage investment and increase international competitiveness. Although this may further increase downward pressure on CIT revenues, it may have positive impacts on future growth prospects. Another factor explaining CIT rate cuts may be the increased focus on measures to counter multinational tax avoidance. These measures will raise the effective tax rates on certain tax aggressive MNEs, which some countries may be aiming to offset through lower CIT rates.

Several countries introduced corporate tax base broadening measures, in particular to protect domestic tax bases against international tax avoidance

Other measures aimed at raising CIT revenues by broadening tax bases. Austria broadened the tax base for certain real estate transactions, raised the applicable tax rate on these transactions and eliminated the educational premium and allowance. To partly counterbalance its substantial rate reductions, Japan's reform package contained several base broadening measures including a simplification of the tax depreciation system, a reduction in the maximum amount of net operating loss deductions that can be carried forward for tax purposes as well as the reduction and elimination of several special tax concessions. Spain removed some tax credits and widened the limits on the deductibility of financial expenses. Hungary implemented a set of anti-avoidance measures including a stricter definition of associated enterprises, limitations to the use of deferred losses in the case of company restructuring, a widening of the minimum profit tax base as well as stricter transfer pricing guidelines.

New taxes and additional revenue-raising corporate provisions were introduced in some countries. Belgium now allows SMEs to assign parts of their profits to a special liquidation reserve. Transfers to the reserve are taxed once at 10% but subsequent distributions benefit from reduced tax rates. This one-off measure is expected to raise just below 0.4% of current GDP in the following four years. In the United Kingdom, the main revenue raising effect is achieved by bringing forward the due dates of corporate tax payments for large corporations and groups by four months. This measure alone is expected to contribute more than 0.2% of current GDP in the first year. Additional revenue-raising measures included bank levies in the United Kingdom and Hungary. Finally, the simplification of the Chilean corporate tax code, which allows taxpayers to choose between totally and partially integrated income taxation, is expected to generate an increase in revenues of around 0.3% of current GDP in four years.

Addressing BEPS was a priority across OECD countries with many countries taking action consistent with the recommendations of the BEPS project. International concern regarding BEPS activities resulted in the launch of the OECD/G20 BEPS project in 2013. In 2015, the final BEPS package was endorsed by OECD and G20 countries. The final package includes recommendations on minimum standards, best practices, common approaches and new guidance in key tax policy areas (see Box 3.3). Several countries have begun introducing anti-avoidance reforms in 2015. Among the base-increasing reforms which were enacted in 2015, a majority aimed at reducing tax avoidance and protecting domestic tax bases from specific tax planning strategies such as the avoidance of permanent establishment (PE) status, transfer mispricing or other forms of profit shifting.

Box 3.3. Recommended policy measures to address BEPS

In October 2015, the final package of BEPS measures was endorsed by G20 leaders in Antalya. The final BEPS package includes recommendations on minimum standards, best practices, common approaches and new guidance in key policy areas.

- Minimum standards have been agreed upon in the areas of fighting harmful tax practices (Action 5), preventing treaty abuse (Action 6), Country-by-Country Reporting (Action 13) and improving dispute resolution (Action 14). All participating countries are expected to implement these minimum standards and implementation will be subject to peer review.
- A common approach, which will facilitate the convergence of national practices by interested countries, has been outlined to limit base erosion through interest expenses (Action 4) and to neutralise hybrid mismatches (Action 2). Best practices for countries which seek to strengthen their domestic legislation are provided on the building blocks for effective CFC rules (Action 3) and mandatory disclosure by taxpayers of aggressive or abusive transactions, arrangements or structures (Action 12).
- The permanent establishment (PE) definition in the OECD Model Tax Convention has been changed to restrict inappropriate avoidance of tax nexus through commissionaire arrangements or exploitation of specific exceptions (Action 7). Follow-up work is being undertaken in 2016 which will also provide further guidance on the attribution of profits to PEs. In terms of transfer pricing, important clarifications have been made with regard to delineating the actual transaction, and the treatment of risk and intangibles. More guidance has been provided on several other issues to ensure that transfer pricing outcomes are aligned with value creation (Actions 8-10).
- The changes to the PE definition, the clarifications on transfer pricing, and the guidance on CFC rules are expected to substantially address the BEPS risks exacerbated by the digital economy. Several other options, including a new nexus in the form of a significant economic presence, were considered, but not recommended at this stage given the other recommendations plus Value Added Taxes (VAT) will now be levied effectively in the market country facilitating VAT collection (Action 1).
- A multilateral instrument will be implemented to facilitate the modification of bilateral tax treaties (Action 15). The modifications made to existing treaties will address the minimum standards against treaty abuse as well as the updated PE definition.

At the February 2016 G20 Finance Ministers meeting, the inclusive framework for the global implementation of the BEPS project was endorsed, with a reiteration of the commitment to timely implementation of the BEPS project and to continue monitoring and addressing BEPS-related issues for a consistent global approach.

Australia and the United Kingdom have implemented measures to address multinational arrangements aimed at avoiding PE status. In January 2016, the Australian multinational anti-avoidance law came into effect, targeting MNEs generating profits in Australia without having a taxable presence in the country. The new law tests whether a non-resident entity derives income from supplying goods or services to Australian residents or whether it avoids the attribution of such income to an Australian PE. If the MNEs activities rely on arrangements which have been designed with the principal purpose of tax avoidance, the respective income will be subject to corporate tax in Australia. Australia also released information on total income, taxable income and tax payable of over 1800 large Australian public, private and foreign private entities for the 2013-14 income year. In the United Kingdom, a new tax on diverted profits, consisting of two complementary rules, took effect in 2015. The first rule addresses arrangements of foreign companies to carry on business in the UK while avoiding PE status. Based on the new law, non-resident companies supplying goods and services to UK residents will pay a 25% tax on profits arising from such transactions. The second rule addresses resident companies and companies with a taxable presence in the UK. Profits earned on the basis of transactions between related entities which fail to meet the economic substance requirements will also be subject to the 25% diverted profit tax. For both rules, a specific provision ensures that UK-based SMEs will not be affected by the new regulations.

Poland introduced Controlled Foreign Company (CFC) rules to counteract profit shifting and the long-term deferral of taxation. Having a controlling interest in a foreign subsidiary may allow parent companies, typically located in high-tax jurisdictions, to assign passive or mobile income, e.g. from intellectual property, services and digital transactions, to low-tax jurisdictions. Several OECD countries already have CFC rules in place to prevent this form of profit shifting. Poland passed a law in 2014 introducing CFC rules as of January 2015. According to this law, foreign companies are considered CFCs if *(a)* they have a registered office or management in a blacklisted jurisdiction, *(b)* they are domiciled in a country with which Poland has not concluded any international convention (e.g. a double taxation treaty), or *(c)* if they meet an ownership threshold of 25% and derive at least 50% of their income from passive income of which at least a part is taxed at a rate of 14.25% or lower. Income from such CFCs is now subject to tax in Poland at a rate of 19%. Poland also introduced significant changes to its transfer pricing regulations in line with the guidelines of the OECD/G20 BEPS Action 13 report to prepare three types of documentation, namely a master file, a local file and a Country-by-Country Report. In parallel, the capital ownership threshold for companies to be considered as related parties was raised from 5% to 25% and will become effective on 1 January 2017, limiting the number of entities that have to submit transfer pricing documentation.

The European Council issued a binding directive to include a general anti-abuse rule (GAAR) in the EU Parent-Subsidiary Directive (PSD). The council directive was passed in January 2015 and corresponding legislative changes must now be implemented in each of the EU member states. The new rules mandate that the benefits of the PSD, withholding tax exemptions for dividends paid by subsidiaries to their parent companies, will not apply anymore to arrangements with the main purpose of tax avoidance.

3.3. VAT/GST and excise duties

Overall, most of the countries that introduced or announced VAT and excise duty reforms in 2015 expect increases in consumption tax revenues. Consumption tax increases were sometimes part of a more comprehensive effort to shift tax burdens away from labour or capital towards consumption (e.g. Belgium and Norway). However, the increase in standard VAT rates, which had been a clear trend since the end of the crisis until the beginning of 2015, did not continue over the course of 2015. In many countries, increases in VAT revenues are expected from reducing the scope of reduced rates and tax compliance improvements. In a number of other countries, VAT revenues are expected to decrease due to the expansion of reduced VAT rates. On cross-border trade in services and intangibles, reforms were also introduced to align tax rules with the OECD International VAT/GST Guidelines. Finally, many countries raised their health-related excise duties.

The increase in standard VAT rates, which had been a clear trend after the crisis, did not continue over the course of 2015

The OECD average standard VAT rate reached an all-time record at the beginning of 2015. Between 2008 and 2015, the average standard VAT rate increased by 1.5 percentage point, from 17.6% to 19.2% (Figure 3.9). While there are significant differences across countries, Figure 3.10 shows that standard VAT rates were raised at least once in 21 OECD countries since 2008, and that 10 countries now have a standard rate above 22%, against only four in 2008. Iceland is the only country where the standard VAT rate has decreased since 2008. Raising the standard VAT rate has been a key part of the approach adopted by many countries since the crisis to consolidate public finances, as VAT rate increases provide immediate revenue impacts, do not directly impact competitiveness and are considered less detrimental to economic growth than direct taxes (OECD, 2010).

However, the trend towards increasing standard VAT rates did not continue over the course of 2015, with an OECD average standard VAT rate in January 2016 at the same level as in 2015

Figure 3.9. **OECD average standard VAT rate, 2000-15**

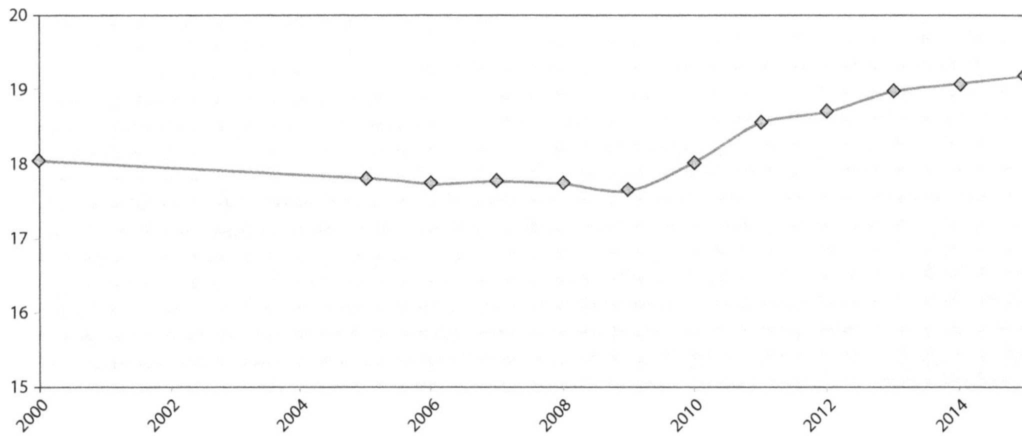

Source: OECD Tax Database, www.oecd.org/tax/tax-policy/tax-database.htm.

Figure 3.10. **Standard VAT rates by country in 2008 and 2015**

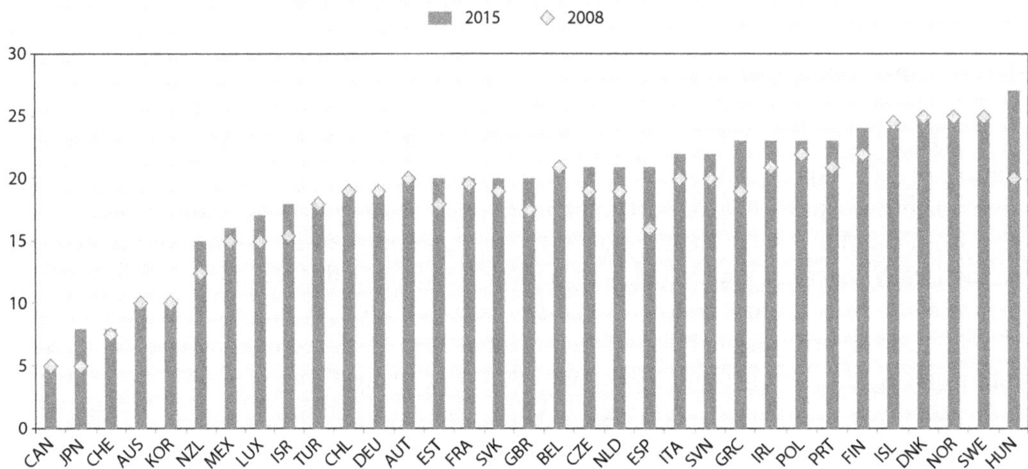

Source: OECD Tax Database, www.oecd.org/tax/tax-policy/tax-database.htm.

(19.2%). In 2015, Luxembourg was the only country that raised its standard VAT rate, from 15% to 17%. On the other hand, Iceland lowered its standard VAT rate from 25.5% to 24% in January and Israel cut its rate from 18% to 17% in October in view of the lower than expected budget deficit and in order to support growth. Few countries have reported plans to change their standard VAT rates in the coming years. Japan confirmed that it still intends to raise its consumption tax to 10% in April 2017.[1] Italy had planned a VAT increase to 24% in 2016 but withdrew it. The new Italian Stability Law introduces potential VAT increases to 24% in 2017 and 25% in 2018 but these will depend on the country's economic performance.

Most countries are expecting revenue increases from consumption tax reforms, in particular through increases in reduced VAT rates, counter-fraud measures and increases in health-related excise duties

Most countries are expecting revenue increases from consumption tax reforms. A number of countries raised their reduced VAT rates or narrowed their scope. These reforms were often in line with the findings and recommendations of the OECD study on the distributional impacts of VAT (OECD/KIPF, 2014) as they focused on scaling back reduced rates that are both inefficient and regressive in the sense that they provide greater benefits to richer households in both aggregate and relative terms. This appears to be the case for Sweden's increased reduced VAT rate on cinema tickets, Austria's increased rate from 10% to 13% for cultural events and accommodation services, and Estonia's increased rate from 9% to 14% on accommodation. In Norway, the reduced VAT rate for transport services and entertainment was raised from 8% to 10% in part to finance the CIT rate cut from 27% to 25%. In Greece, the scope of the 13% reduced VAT rate was significantly narrowed to respond to the demands of its bailout agreement with the EC, the ECB and the IMF. Over 100 types of goods and services, including sugar, coffee, beef, spices, oil for cooking and salt, became subject to the standard rate of 23%. The VAT increase also included a shift from the super-reduced to the reduced rate for hotel accommodation and the gradual withdrawal of the scheme granting reduced rates on the Aegean Islands.

Other VAT base broadening reforms include Australia's extension of GST to imported goods valued at or below AUD 1 000. This measure was announced in August 2015 and will become effective on 1 July 2017. It will subject low-value goods imported by consumers to the same tax regime as goods that are produced domestically as well as generate an additional AUD 300 million in GST revenues between 2017 and 2020. Overseas suppliers that have an Australian turnover of AUD 75 000 or more will be required to register for, collect and remit GST for low value goods supplied to consumers in Australia. With this reform, Australia is a first mover on applying GST to low-value imported goods.

Several countries reported the introduction of measures to counter VAT fraud. Many European countries extended the domestic reverse charge mechanism (i.e. shifting the obligation to declare and pay VAT from the supplier to the purchaser) in sectors subject to high risks of fraud (e.g. construction in the Slovak Republic, agricultural crops in Czech Republic, the wholesale supply of gas and electricity in Ireland). The reverse charge mechanism is intended to combat "missing trader fraud" – which involves fraudsters importing goods VAT-free from other EU countries and then selling them domestically with a VAT charge that they do not remit to tax authorities – or complex versions of this type of fraud relying on many dummy companies known as "carousel fraud". Additional measures to tackle VAT evasion that were reported included VAT control statements which request detailed information on the taxable supplies made and/or received in the country (Czech Republic) and the use or extension of cash registers that transmit data electronically to revenue authorities (Hungary, Slovenia).

With regard to excise duties, many countries reported increases in their health-related taxes. Tobacco and alcohol taxes were raised in a significant number of countries either simply to adjust for inflation (e.g. Estonia, New Zealand) or to deter unhealthy consumption (e.g. Belgium, Hungary, Ireland). In the Netherlands, the tax rate on soft drinks was raised. In Belgium, a new health tax on sugary drinks was introduced, taking effect in January 2016. This measure was part of a broader effort to shift the tax mix away from labour towards consumption taxes.

In other countries, VAT revenues are expected to decrease due to base narrowing provisions

In other countries, reforms are expected to reduce consumption tax revenues. Several countries lowered their reduced VAT rates or increased their scope, mostly for distributional reasons. The justification for lowering reduced rates or expanding their scope in these countries was primarily to help the poor (e.g. lower VAT rates on selected foodstuffs in the Slovak Republic and Hungary) and to support families (e.g. lower VAT rates on newly-built homes in Hungary). Concerns about the distributional effects of the standard VAT rate increase on low-income people also pushed Japan to announce the introduction of an 8% reduced VAT rate on food and newspapers in 2017.[2] In France, the Parliament approved a VAT rate cut from 20% to 5.5% on sanitary products, making their tax treatment equivalent to that of essential items. Lowering VAT on sanitary products was also discussed in Australia and the United Kingdom. In other cases, the expansion of reduced VAT rates was motivated by non-distributional objectives. For instance, the Czech Republic announced a VAT rate cut on restaurant services effective in December 2016, indirectly providing support to this sector.

Some countries introduced reforms to simplify VAT compliance

Some countries introduced reforms to simplify VAT compliance and in particular to lower the administrative burden on SMEs. In Greece, Belgium and Finland, the VAT registration thresholds were raised. The Slovak Republic introduced simplified conditions for faster VAT refunds and a cash accounting scheme for businesses with a yearly turnover below EUR 100 000 which postpones the obligation to remit VAT until the customer's payment is received. In Slovenia, the process for charging and paying VAT on imports was simplified: importers will no longer be required to pay VAT when they import goods but will instead make their VAT payment through a VAT return for the tax period in which the goods were imported.

Reforms were introduced to align rules with the OECD International VAT/GST Guidelines

The release of the OECD International VAT/GST Guidelines (the "Guidelines") in November 2015 was a major international tax development (Box 3.4). The elements of the Guidelines that received most attention since their release were the recommended rules and mechanisms for the effective collection of VAT on business-to-consumer (B2C) supplies of services and intangibles (including digital supplies) by foreign suppliers. The Guidelines recommend that the right to tax these supplies for VAT purposes be allocated to the country where the private customer has its usual residence and that foreign suppliers of these services and intangibles register and remit VAT in the country of the customer's usual residence. The Guidelines recommend the implementation of a simplified registration and compliance regime to facilitate compliance for foreign suppliers.

Box 3.4. OECD International VAT/GST Guidelines

At the November 2015 OECD Global Forum on VAT, more than 100 countries and jurisdictions endorsed the new OECD International VAT/GST Guidelines as the international standard to ensure a coherent and efficient application of VAT/GST to international trade in services.

In the absence of these Guidelines, there was no internationally agreed framework for the application of VAT to cross-border trade, in contrast with existing frameworks for the taxation of income such as the OECD Model Tax Convention and the Transfer Pricing Guidelines. This led to increasing uncertainty and complexity for both tax authorities and businesses and risks of double taxation and unintended non-taxation. This was a matter of special concern with respect to international trade in services and intangibles, which has considerably increased over the last decade.

The Guidelines include chapters on the principle of VAT neutrality and its implementation in practice, and on the implementation of the destination principle for allocating the taxing rights on cross-border supplies of services and intangibles.

For business-to-business supplies the Guidelines establish that, the taxing rights on cross-border supplies of services and intangibles are to be allocated to the jurisdiction where the business customer has located its permanent business presence. For business-to-consumer supplies, the Guidelines recommend that the taxing rights over "on-the-spot supplies" be allocated to the jurisdiction in which the supply is physically performed; and that the taxing rights over all other supplies and services be allocated to the jurisdiction in which the customer has its usual residence. These include remote supplies of services and digital products over the Internet (e.g. apps, streaming of music and movies, online gaming) by foreign suppliers. The Guidelines recommend that these foreign suppliers be required to register and remit VAT in the jurisdiction of taxation and that countries implement a simplified registration and compliance regime to facilitate compliance for non-resident suppliers.

The Guidelines do not aim at providing detailed prescriptions for national legislation. Jurisdictions are sovereign with respect to the design and application of their laws. Rather, the Guidelines seek to identify objectives and suggest means for achieving them, thereby serving as a reference point. Global Forum participants urged the OECD and G20 to develop implementation packages to support the consistent implementation of the Guidelines and to design an even more inclusive framework that would involve all interested countries and jurisdictions, particularly developing countries, on an equal footing.

Reforms were introduced to align tax rules on cross-border trade in services and intangibles with the Guidelines. A number of OECD countries had already implemented such an approach, including most notably the 28 EU member states (under the EU VAT framework) and Norway. Other OECD countries have made progress in implementing the Guidelines. Japan and Korea both implemented them in 2015 while New Zealand and Australia are planning their implementation respectively for late 2016 and 2017. These changes are expected to remove distortions between domestic and foreign digital service suppliers as well as broaden VAT bases.

Changes in VAT bases and the fight against VAT fraud will likely have an impact on countries' VAT Revenue Ratios. The VAT Revenue Ratio (VRR) is the ratio between the revenue collected from VAT and the revenue that would be raised if the standard VAT rate were applied uniformly to all final consumption, with perfect tax enforcement. In other words, the VRR combines the degree to which VAT policy is designed to tax consumption at a uniform rate together with the quality of compliance and tax administration. Figure 3.11

shows that VRRs varied quite significantly across OECD countries in 2012. In the future, some of the countries that have implemented reforms that either broaden VAT bases or strengthen VAT enforcement may experience improvements in their VRR (e.g. Greece, Norway, Slovenia), while others, where VAT bases were narrowed or where tax enforcement issues are prevalent, could see their VRR deteriorate.

Figure 3.11. **VAT Revenue Ratios in OECD countries**

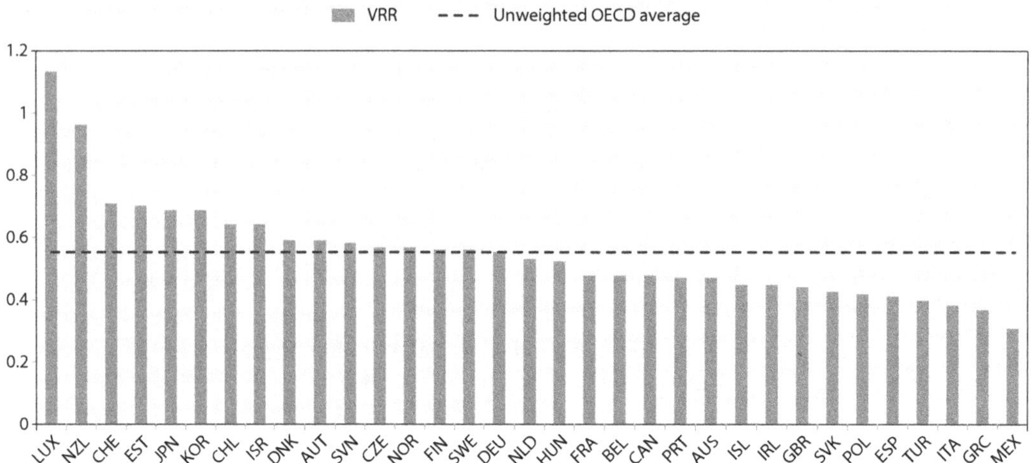

Note: Based on figures for 2012.

Source: OECD (2014a), *Consumption Tax Trends 2014: VAT/GST and excise rates, trends and policy issues*, http://dx.doi.org/10.1787/ctt-2014-en.

3.4. Environmentally related taxes

Overall, environmentally related tax reforms in 2015 concentrated on transport fuel and vehicle taxation. Stated rationales pertained to revenue-raising and environmental objectives in roughly equal measure. Changes in transport fuel taxation resulted in a smaller gap between diesel and petrol taxation in some countries, reducing the adverse environmental signal from taxing diesel less per litre than petrol. Changes in vehicle taxes took the form of reductions in a few countries but in most cases sought to encourage the purchase of less polluting vehicles (on a CO_2 or NO_x emission basis) or alternative fuel vehicles. These reforms are expected to somewhat improve the environmental effectiveness of taxes and to generate small revenue increases in some countries in the short term but they are unlikely to reverse the long-run decline in revenues from environmentally related taxes.

Climate policy was high on the agenda but carbon emissions remain largely under-priced

Environmentally related taxes include all taxes that are likely to have a strong environmental impact, regardless of the reason why they were introduced. Across OECD countries, environmentally related taxes raised revenue amounting to approximately 2.2% of GDP in 2014 (Figure 3.12), which is less than in 2000, when the share was around 2.5%. Environmentally related tax revenue as a share of GDP fell in most countries. The countries where the share increased are now among the ones with the highest shares, noting that some of these countries were in the middle range in 2000 (e.g. Turkey and Italy). The inter-country differences in revenue shares were more pronounced in 2014 than in 2000.

The declining shares of revenues from environmentally related taxes and the increase in inter-country differences are likely due to at least three factors. First, they are partly the consequence of the fact that environmentally related taxes usually take the form of excise taxes and that not all countries maintain real tax rate levels. Second, the economic crisis and crude oil price rises (through their impact on fuel prices) depressed the environmentally related tax base. Third, while increasing environmentally related tax rates may increase revenues in the short and medium term, they may lead to a decrease in harmful emissions, thereby reducing the tax base over time and possibly the revenues resulting from them. In addition, other environmental policies may overlap with environmentally related taxes and reduce tax bases.

Figure 3.12. **Revenue from environmentally related taxes in 2014 and 2000, in % of GDP, OECD countries**

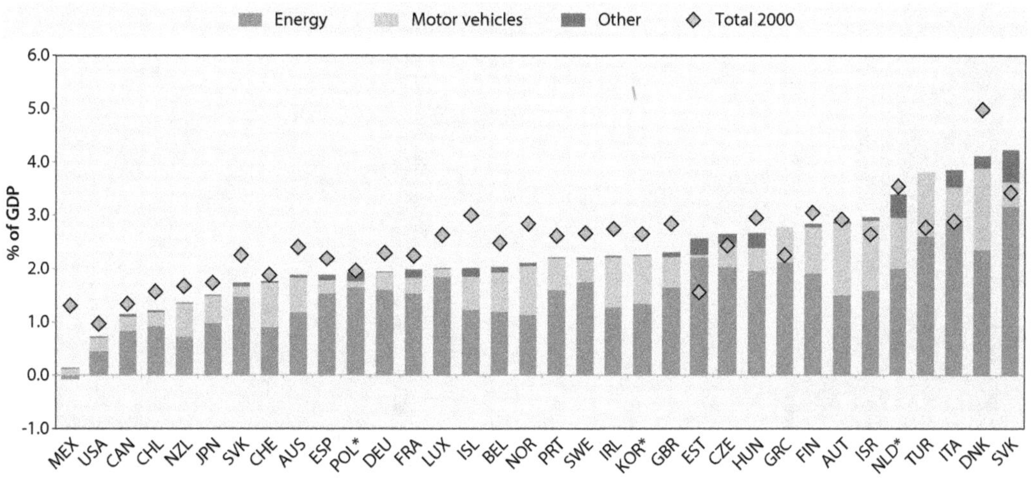

* 2013 figures for Poland, Korea and the Netherlands.

Source: OECD (2016b), Database on instruments used for environmental policy, http://www2.oecd.org/ecoinst/queries/.

Taxes on energy use continue to be the largest source of environmentally related tax revenue by far, exceeding those on motor vehicles and other taxes (Figure 3.12). Within the category of taxes on energy use, revenues from taxes on transport fuels are predominant. This reflects the frequent taxation of the use of oil products and typically high transport fuel tax rates. Non-oil forms of energy are less often taxed, or are taxed at lower rates. Figure 3.13 shows a graphical profile of average effective tax rates (y axis) and energy use (x axis) across the main fuel categories for total energy use in 41 OECD and G20 countries. The Figure shows clear differences between road transport fuel and other energy taxes, and particularly low taxes on some of the most environmentally harmful fuels (notably coal). Taxes on energy use are often not aligned with the environmental costs of energy use, so the potential for harnessing the power of taxes as environmental policy instruments is large.

Climate policy was high on the agenda in 2015 with the United Nations climate change conference (COP21) held in Paris in December. COP21 delivered beyond expectations. The Paris Agreement is a milestone in international efforts to craft an effective response to climate change. It aims to hold the global average temperature increase to well below 2°C and to pursue efforts to limit it to 1.5°C (UNFCCC, 2015). To reach these goals, the world economy needs to fully decarbonise in the second half of this century. The reduction of emissions in a cost-effective way calls for the use of carbon prices, i.e. taxes and emissions trading systems. The Paris Agreement allows for the use of such instruments but does not in itself encourage the use of particular instruments. The momentum will need to emerge from countries or coalitions of countries.

Figure 3.13. **Graphical profile of energy use and taxation across all energy use in 41 OECD and G20 countries (weighted average basis), 2012**

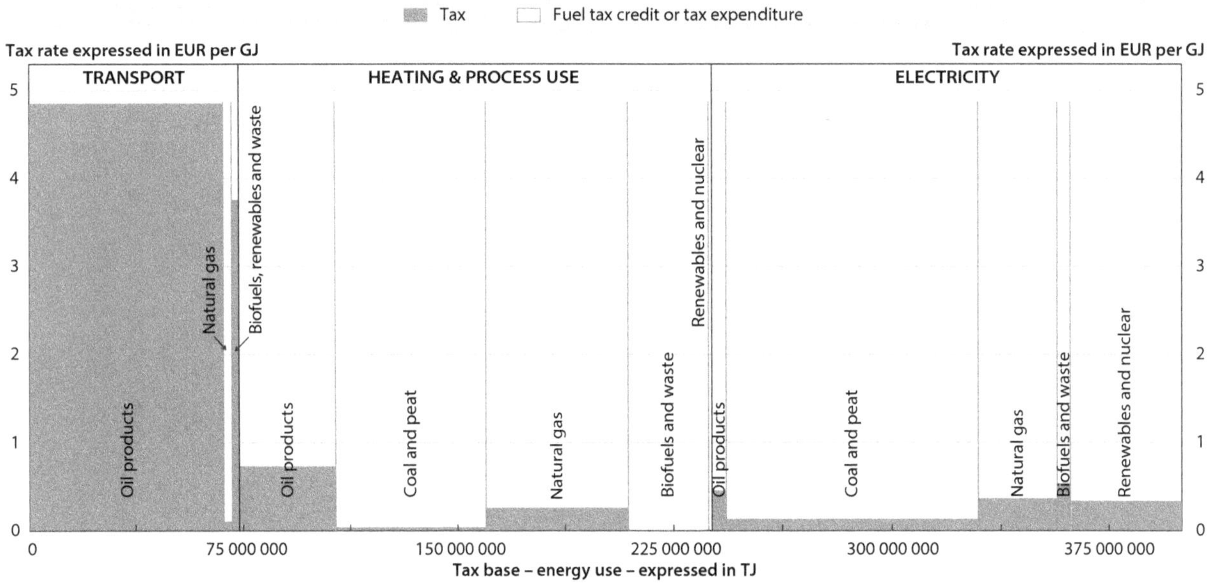

Source: OECD (2015b), *Taxing Energy Use: OECD and selected Partner economies*, http://dx.doi.org/10.1787/9789264232334-en.

Carbon prices are currently low and heterogeneous, resulting in limited incentives for cost-effective abatement. This was highlighted by the OECD analysis of effective carbon rates, which are calculated as the sum of price signals resulting from specific energy taxes (excise taxes), carbon taxes and prices of tradable emission permits, expressed in EUR per tonne of CO_2. Effective carbon rates of EUR 30 per tonne of CO_2 reflect a conservative estimate of the climate damage resulting from a tonne of emissions. Figure 3.14 shows the distribution of effective carbon rates across 41 OECD and G20 countries. In road transport, which contributes to 15 % of CO_2 emissions from energy use in those 41 countries, most countries already price the vast majority of their emissions above EUR 30 per tonne of CO_2. However, in the non-road sectors, which make up 85% of emissions, only very few countries price CO_2 emissions above EUR 30 per tonne. Overall, 90% of emissions are priced below EUR 30 per tonne of CO_2. For non-road emissions, the share is 96%.

There are signs that carbon pricing instruments are increasingly being used. The World Bank reports that approximately 12% of greenhouse gas emissions were covered by carbon taxes or emissions trading systems in 2015, compared to less than 5% up to 2012, and less than 1% up to 2005 (Kossoy et al., 2015). Further indications of such a dynamic include the Chinese decision to move to a nationwide emissions trading system (although this may be delayed), discussions on carbon taxation in several US states and on emission trading systems and carbon taxation in Canadian provinces. This increased coverage is a step in the right direction but it will ultimately need to be accompanied by rising rates if carbon pricing is to fully achieve its potential.

Figure 3.14. **Share of CO_2 emissions subject to different effective carbon rates in EUR per tonne**

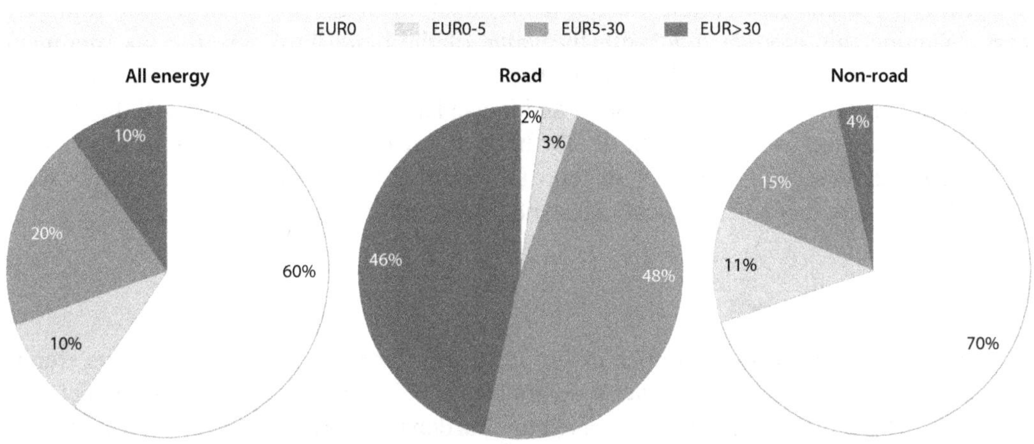

Source: OECD (2015c), *Effective Carbon Rates on Energy: OECD and selected Partner Economies*, http://www.oecd.org/tax/tax-policy/effective-carbon-rates-on-energy.pdf.

Environmentally related tax reforms in 2015 focused on taxes on transport fuels and vehicles

In addition to the activity observed on emissions trading and explicit carbon taxes, six countries increased their excise taxes on fuels in 2015 stating both revenue raising and environmental objectives as rationales for the reforms. France, Estonia and Portugal both increased taxes on transport and heating fuels. Finland increased the CO_2-component of its taxes on heating fuels thereby increasing overall rates, and New Zealand and Sweden increased their taxes on transport fuels. These reforms are expected to somewhat improve the environmental effectiveness of these taxes. While Hungary increased energy tax rates to comply with EU minimum tax rates, it also implemented an energy tax refund for some manufacturing companies, which is expected overall to lead to a small decrease in revenues from energy taxes. As part of a comprehensive tax reform, the Netherlands increased taxes on natural gas used for heating, decreased taxes on electricity for small users and reintroduced a tax exemption for coal used for electricity generation, leading to a revenue increase in overall terms.

Two countries, Belgium and France increased excise taxes on diesel while lowering those on petrol, resulting in a narrower tax differential between both fuels. The overall revenue impact is expected to be positive for Belgium. Narrowing the tax differential between diesel and gasoline will also better reflect environmental costs as diesel emits higher levels of carbon dioxide per litre than gasoline and, depending on the technology employed, often also more harmful air pollutants (Harding, 2014).

Changes in vehicle taxes took the form of reductions in a few countries, but these measures generally aimed at encouraging the purchase of less polluting vehicles (on a CO_2 or NO_x emission basis) or alternative fuel vehicles. Both Denmark and Finland lowered overall registration taxes on vehicles. It should be noted that in both countries the reductions constitute decreases from relatively high starting points. Denmark also fully exempted alternative fuel vehicles from the registration tax in 2015 but this exemption expired on 1 January 2016 and alternative fuel vehicles will be progressively phased into the regular registration tax system. Chile introduced a tax on vehicle registrations that varies with urban performance (km/litre), NO_x emissions and sale price, and the United Kingdom announced that it will adjust registration taxes according to CO_2 performance standards from 2017 onwards.

Austria, Estonia and Korea increased the taxation of the personal use of company cars, bringing this more in line with the value of the benefit. Where the tax treatment of company cars does not fully capture this benefit, this entails a fiscal cost and can encourage users to drive cars more often and to use larger vehicles (OECD, 2014b). Austria linked the increase in taxable benefits to the CO_2 performance standards of the vehicle in order to decrease emissions. Other reported environmentally related tax reforms were limited to tax rate increases on pesticides and gravel in Sweden.

3.5. Property taxes

Overall, only a limited number of property tax reforms were reported. The trends across OECD countries in 2015 were also unclear, except in the area of inheritance and gift taxes where three countries decreased tax burdens. Reforms were motivated by very different objectives, such as revenue generation or containing housing prices when taxes were raised, or increasing households' disposable incomes when they were lowered. One of the most significant reforms adopted in 2015 was the abolition of the local service tax on primary residences in Italy. This section suggests that the potential to raise revenues in an efficient way through property taxes, especially through recurrent taxes on residential property, has not been fully exploited. The relatively limited number of reforms confirms that property taxes remain particularly difficult to reform and continue to face significant political economy constraints.

There were only a limited number of reforms in the area of property taxes

OECD countries impose a range of taxes on property. Most prominent are recurrent taxes on immovable property, which are typically a key source of revenue for local government. Inheritance, gift and property transaction taxes are also common in OECD countries. A smaller number of countries impose a tax on some measure of net wealth. Nevertheless, property taxes account for a small share of total tax revenues across the OECD. Even if total property tax revenues varied quite widely across OECD countries, they accounted on average for only 1.9% of GDP in OECD countries in 2013 (Figure 3.15).

In 2015, Finland and Italy were the only two countries that reported reforms in the area of recurrent taxes on immovable property. Finland introduced a gradual increase in the maximum recurrent real estate tax rates in 2016 to boost municipalities' revenues. Italy, on the other hand, abolished its property tax for local services (TASI) on primary residences, except for luxury houses. Following the elimination of the municipal tax (IMU) on primary residences in 2014, the abolition of TASI means that the local tax on environmental and waste services (TARI) is the only remaining tax on primary residences. This reform was primarily motivated by distributional concerns as home ownership was argued to be widespread in Italy with a large share of home owners being workers and pensioners. However, the reform goes against a pro-growth shift in the tax mix towards taxes that were found to be less distortive than other taxes (OECD, 2010). The budget cost of the reform is estimated to be around EUR 3.5 billion per year.

Figure 3.15. **Property tax revenues as a share of GDP in 2014**

Note: 2013 data for Australia, Greece, Mexico, the Netherlands and Poland.

Source: OECD (2015), *Revenue Statistics 2015*, http://dx.doi.org/10.1787/rev_stats-2015-en-fr.

Some changes were made to transaction taxes on immovable property. In Israel, a temporary measure was introduced until 2020 to raise the tax rates for buyers owning more than one apartment. This tax increase is expected to contain housing prices – which more than doubled between 2008 and 2015 – by reducing the demand from investors (i.e. people who already own more than one flat). In the United Kingdom, the government announced a 3% surcharge on the Stamp Duty Land Tax from April 2016 for people purchasing additional residential properties, targeting in particular buy-to-let landlords. In Austria, the real estate transaction tax was raised through a change in the tax base for unremunerated real estate transfers within families from a favourable cadastre value to the market value. To some extent, this is comparable to the introduction of a gift tax on real estate transfers within families. In addition, in the case of unremunerated real estate transfers, the uniform tax rate was replaced with a schedule with three brackets depending on transaction values. For transfers of real estate used for business, the tax burden was reduced through an increase in the tax-free allowance.

Some reforms were also introduced in countries that impose recurrent taxes on net wealth. In Spain, the recurrent tax on net wealth that was re-introduced in 2011 as a temporary measure was extended again in 2016 to further consolidate public finances. In Norway, the net wealth tax burden was reduced through an increase in the basic allowance.

With regard to inheritance and gift taxes, three countries reported changes, all lowering tax burdens by narrowing tax bases. In October 2015, Ireland raised the tax-free threshold of its gift and inheritance tax by almost 25%. In December 2015, the Netherlands enacted a reform that will reduce its gift tax by nearly doubling the exemption for a gift intended for the purchase or the improvement of owner-occupied property. As of January 2017, this exemption will amount to EUR 100 000. In addition, the limiting condition that the gift must be from a parent to a child will be removed, meaning that the tax exemption will be available for gifts outside of the family. However, the condition that the beneficiary be aged between 18 and 40 will still apply. Finally, the United Kingdom announced the introduction of an additional tax-free band under the inheritance tax for the transfer on death of a residence to a direct descendant as from 2017.

Notes

1. In June 2016, the Japanese Prime Minister announced that the consumption tax rate increase to 10% would be postponed until October 2019.

2. In June 2016, the Japanese Prime Minister announced that the reduced VAT rate would be introduced at the same time as the standard VAT rate increase in October 2019.

Sources

Brys, B., S. Perret, A. Thomas and P. O'Reilly (forthcoming, 2016), "Tax Design for Inclusive Economic Growth", *OECD Taxation Working Papers*, OECD Publishing, Paris.

Harding, M. (2014), "The Diesel Differential: Differences in the Tax Treatment of Gasoline and Diesel for Road Use", *OECD Taxation Working Papers*, No. 21, OECD Publishing, Paris, http://dx.doi.org/10.1787/5jz14cd7hk6b-en.

Harding, M. (2013), "Taxation of Dividend, Interest, and Capital Gain Income", *OECD Taxation Working Papers*, No. 19, OECD Publishing, http://dx.doi.org/10.1787/5k3wh96w246k-en.

Kopczuk, W. (2005), "Tax Bases, Tax Rates and the Elasticity of Reported Income," *Journal of Public Economics*, 89(11-12), 2093-2119.

OECD (2016a), *Taxing Wages 2016*, OECD Publishing, Paris, http://dx.doi.org/10.1787/tax_wages-2016-en.

OECD (2016b), Database on instruments used for environmental policy, http://www2.oecd.org/ecoinst/queries/.

OECD. (2015a), *Revenue Statistics 2015*, OECD Publishing, Paris, http://dx.doi.org/10.1787/rev_stats-2015-en-fr.

OECD (2015b), *Taxing Energy Use: OECD and selected Partner economies,* OECD Publishing, Paris, http://dx.doi.org/10.1787/9789264232334-en.

OECD (2015c), *Effective Carbon Rates on Energy: OECD and selected Partner Economies*, OECD, Paris, http://www.oecd.org/tax/tax-policy/effective-carbon-rates-on-energy.pdf.

OECD/KIPF (2014), *The Distributional Effects of Consumption Taxes in OECD Countries*, OECD Tax Policy Studies, No. 22, OECD Publishing, Paris, http://dx.doi.org/10.1787/9789264224520-en.

OECD (2014a), *Consumption Tax Trends 2014: VAT/GST and excise rates, trends and policy issues*, OECD Publishing, Paris, http://dx.doi.org/10.1787/ctt-2014-en.

OECD (2014b), "Tax benefits from company cars: A driver of social costs. Policy Highlights" (brochure), OECD, Paris.

OECD (2011), *Taxation and Employment*, OECD Tax Policy Studies, No. 21, OECD Publishing, http://dx.doi.org/10.1787/9789264120808-en.

OECD (2010), *Tax Policy Reform and Economic Growth*, OECD Tax Policy Studies, No. 20, OECD Publishing, Paris, http://dx.doi.org/10.1787/9789264091085-en.

UNFCCC (2015), "Adoption of the Paris Agreement", FCCC/CP/2015/L.9?Rev.1.

Annex A

Changes to the taxation of earned income made or announced in 2015

	Personal income taxes: earned income							
	Top rate	Non-top rate	Personal allowances, credits, tax brackets	Targeted low income/EITCs	Children & other dependents	Elderly & disabled	Miscellaneous deductions	Education
Australia				Broadening				
Austria	Increase	Decrease		Narrowing	Narrowing		Broadening	
Belgium	Decrease	Decrease		Narrowing			Narrowing	
Canada								
Chile								
Czech Republic								
Denmark								
Estonia	Decrease	Decrease			Broadening			Broadening
Finland			Narrowing					
France		Decrease		Narrowing				
Germany			Narrowing		Narrowing			
Greece								
Hungary	Decrease							
Iceland		Decrease						
Ireland		Decrease			Narrowing			
Israel								
Italy								
Japan								
Korea								
Luxembourg								
Mexico			Narrowing					
Netherlands		Decrease	Broadening	Narrowing	Narrowing	Narrowing		
New Zealand								
Norway		Decrease						
Poland								
Portugal								
Slovak Republic				Narrowing				
Slovenia								
Spain	Decrease	Decrease	Narrowing					
Sweden			Broadening	Narrowing		Narrowing	Broadening	Broadening
Switzerland							Broadening	
Turkey					Narrowing			Narrowing
United Kingdom								
United States				Narrowing	Narrowing			Narrowing

ORGANISATION FOR ECONOMIC CO-OPERATION AND DEVELOPMENT

The OECD is a unique forum where governments work together to address the economic, social and environmental challenges of globalisation. The OECD is also at the forefront of efforts to understand and to help governments respond to new developments and concerns, such as corporate governance, the information economy and the challenges of an ageing population. The Organisation provides a setting where governments can compare policy experiences, seek answers to common problems, identify good practice and work to co-ordinate domestic and international policies.

The OECD member countries are: Australia, Austria, Belgium, Canada, Chile, the Czech Republic, Denmark, Estonia, Finland, France, Germany, Greece, Hungary, Iceland, Ireland, Israel, Italy, Japan, Korea, Latvia, Luxembourg, Mexico, the Netherlands, New Zealand, Norway, Poland, Portugal, the Slovak Republic, Slovenia, Spain, Sweden, Switzerland, Turkey, the United Kingdom and the United States. The European Union takes part in the work of the OECD.

OECD Publishing disseminates widely the results of the Organisation's statistics gathering and research on economic, social and environmental issues, as well as the conventions, guidelines and standards agreed by its members.

OECD PUBLISHING, 2, rue André-Pascal, 75775 PARIS CEDEX 16
(23 2016 31 1 P) ISBN 978-92-64-26037-5 – 2016

www.ingramcontent.com/pod-product-compliance
Lightning Source LLC
LaVergne TN
LVHW081423110826
845149LV00010B/1847

* 9 7 8 9 2 6 4 2 6 0 3 7 5 *